THE TEACHING
OF
BUDDHA

THE TEACHINGS
OF
BUDDHA

BUKKYŌ DENDŌ KYŌKAI

A Sterling Paperback

STERLING PAPERBACKS
An imprint of
Sterling Publishers (P) Ltd.
A-59 Okhla Industrial Area, Phase-II,
New Delhi-110020.
Tel: 26387070, 26386209; Fax: 91-11-26383788
E-mail: info@sterlingpublishers.com
Website: www.sterlingpublishers.com

Sole distributors in Sri Lanka, Singapore and Malaysia
Buddhist Cultural Centre
125 Anderson Road, Nedimala,
Dehiwala, Sri Lanka
Tel: + 94 11-2734256, 2728468, Fax: 2736737

The Teachings of Buddha
© 2004, Bukkyō Dendō Kyōkai
First Edition, 2004
ISBN 81 207 2781 9
Reprint 2006

All rights are reserved. No part of this publication may be reproduced,
stored in a retrieval system or transmitted, in any form or by any
means, mechanical, photocopying, recording or otherwise, without
prior written permission of the publisher.

Published by Sterling Publishers Pvt. Ltd., New Delhi-110020.
Lasertypeset by Vikas Compographics, New Delhi-110020.
Printed at Sai Early Learners Pvt. Ltd, New Delhi-110020

Wheel of Dharma

The Wheel of Dharma is the translation of the Sanskrit word, "Dharma-chakra." Similar to the wheel of a cart that keeps revolving, it symbolises the Buddha's teachings as it continues to be spread widely and endlessly. The eight spokes of the wheel represent the Noble Eightfold Path of Buddhism, the most important way of practice. The Noble Eightfold Path refers to right view, right thought, right speech, right behaviour, right livelihood, right effort, right mindfulness, and right meditation. In the olden days before statues and other images of the Buddha were made, this Wheel of Dharma served as the object of worship. At present, the Wheel is used internationally as the common symbol of Buddhism.

******

Buddha's Wisdom is broad as the ocean and His Spirit is full of great Compassion.

Buddha has no form but manifests Himself in exquisiteness and leads us with His whole heart full of Compassion.

This book is valuable because it contains the essence of the Buddha's teachings as recorded in over five thousand volumes. These teachings have been preserved and handed down for more than twenty-five hundred years extending beyond borders and racial barriers of the world.

The words of Buddha contained in this book touch on all aspects of human life and bring meaning to it.

Dhammapada

Hatred never ceases by hatred in this world. By love alone they cease. This is an ancient law.

A fool who thinks that he is a fool is for that very reason a wise man. The fool who thinks that he is wise is a fool indeed.

Though he should live a hundred years, not seeing the Truth Sublime; yet better, indeed, is the single day's life of one who sees the Truth Sublime.

Hard is birth as man, Hard is the life of mortals, Hard is the hearing of the Sublime Truth, Hard is the appearance of a Buddha.

Not to do any evil, to cultivate good, to purify one's mind, – This is the advice of the Buddhas.

There are no sons for protection, neither father nor even kinsmen; for him who is overcome by death no protection is there from kinsmen.

Contents

Part – III
THE WAY OF PRACTICE

Part – IV
THE BROTHERHOOD

Part – I
BUDDHA

Part – 1
BUDDHA

Chapter One

Shakyamuni Buddha

I

The Life of the Buddha

1. The Shakya clansmen dwelt along the Rohini river which flows among the southern foothills of the Himalayas. Their king, Shuddhodana Gautama, established his capital at Kapilavastu, had a great castle built there and ruled wisely, winning the acclaim of his people.

The queen's name was Maya. She was the daughter of the king's uncle who was also the king of a neighbouring district of the same Shakya clan.

For twenty years they had no children. But one night queen Maya had a strange dream, in which she saw a white elephant entering into her womb through the right side of her chest, and she became pregnant. The king and the people looked forward with anticipation to the birth of a royal child. According to their custom the queen returned to her parents' home for the birth, and on her way, in the beautiful spring sunshine, she took a rest in the Lumbini Garden.

All about her were Ashoka blossoms. In delight she reached her right arm out to pluck a branch and as she did so a prince was born. All expressed their heartfelt delight with the glory of the queen and her princely child; heaven and earth rejoiced. This memorable day was the eighth day of April.

The joy of the king was extreme and he named the child, Siddhartha, which means "Every wish fulfilled."

2. In the palace of the king, however, delight was followed quickly by sorrow, for after several days the lovely queen Maya suddenly died. Her younger sister, Mahaprajapati, became the child's foster mother and brought him up with loving care.

A hermit, called Asita, who lived in the mountains not far away, noticed a radiance about the castle. Interpreting it as a good omen he came down to the palace and was shown the child. He predicted: "This prince, if he remains in the palace, when grown up will become a great king and subjugate the whole world. But if he forsakes the court life to embrace a religious life, he will become a Buddha, the Saviour of the world."

At first the king was pleased to hear this prophecy, but later he started to worry about the possibility of his only son leaving the palace to become a homeless recluse.

At the age of seven the prince began his lessons in the civil and military arts, but his thoughts more naturally tended to other things. One spring day he went out of the castle with his father. Together they were watching a farmer plowing his field when he noticed a bird descending to the ground and carrying off a small worm which had been turned up by the farmer's plough. He sat down in the shade of a tree and thought about it, whispering to himself:

"Alas! Do all living creatures kill each other?"

The prince, who had lost his mother soon after his birth, was deeply affected by the tragedy of these little creatures.

This spiritual wound deepened day by day as he grew up; like a little scar on a young tree, the suffering of human life became more and more deeply engrained in his mind.

The king was increasingly worried as he recalled the hermit's prophecy and tried in every possible way to cheer the prince and to turn his thoughts in other directions. The king arranged the marriage of the prince at the age of nineteen to the Princess Yashodhara. She was the daughter of Suprabuddha, the Lord of Devadaha Castle and a brother of the late queen Maya.

3. For ten years, in the different Pavilions of Spring, Autumn and the Rainy Season, the prince was immersed in rounds of music, dancing and pleasure, but his thoughts always returned to the problem of suffering as he pensively tried to understand the true meaning of human life.

"The luxuries of the palace, this healthy body, this rejoicing youth! What do they mean to me?" He thought. "Some day we may be sick, we shall become aged; from death there is no escape. Pride of youth, pride of health, pride of existence – all thoughtful people should cast them aside.

"A man struggling for existence will naturally look for something of value. There are two ways of looking – a right way and a wrong way. If he looks in the wrong way he recognises that sickness, old age and death are unavoidable, but he seeks the opposite.

"If he looks in the right way he recognises the true nature of sickness, old age and death, and he searches for meaning in that which transcends all human sufferings. In my life of pleasures I seem to be looking in the wrong way."

4. Thus the spiritual struggle went on in the mind of the prince until his only child, Rahula, was born when he was 29. This seemed to bring things to a climax, for he then decided to leave the palace and look for the solution of his spiritual unrest in the homeless life of a mendicant. He left the castle one night with only his charioteer, Chandaka, and his favourite horse, the snow-white Kanthaka.

His anguish did not end and many devils tempted him saying: "You would do better to return to the castle for the whole world would soon be yours." But he told the devil that he did not want the whole world. So he shaved his head and turned his steps toward the south, carrying a begging bowl in his hand.

The prince first visited the hermit Bhagava and watched his ascetic practices. He then went to Arada Kalama and Udraka Ramaputra to learn their methods of attaining Enlightenment through meditation; but after practising them for a while he became convinced that they would not lead him to Enlightenment. Finally he went to the land of Magadha and practised asceticism in the forest of Uruvilva on the banks of the Nairanjana river, which flows by the Gaya village.

5. The methods of his practice were unbelievably rigorous. He spurred, himself on with the thought that "no ascetic in the past, none in the present, and none in the future, ever has practised or ever will practise more earnestly than I do."

Still the prince could not realise his goal. After six years in the forest he gave up the practice of asceticism. He went bathing in the river and accepted a bowl of milk from the hand of Sujata, a maiden, who lived in the neighbouring village. The five companions who had lived with the prince during the six years of his ascetic practice were shocked that he should receive milk from the hand of a maiden; they thought him degraded and left him.

Thus the prince was left alone. He was still weak, but at the risk of losing his life he attempted yet another period of meditation, saying to himself, "Blood may become exhausted, flesh may decay, bones may fall apart, but I will never leave this place until I find the way to Enlightenment."

It was an intense and incomparable struggle for him. He was desperate and filled with confusing thoughts, dark shadows overhung his spirit, and he was beleaguered by all the lures of the devils. Carefully and patiently he examined them one by one and rejected them all. It was a hard struggle indeed, making his blood run thin, his flesh fall away, and his bones crack.

But when the morning star appeared in the eastern sky, the struggle was over and the prince's mind was as clear and bright as the breaking day. He had, at last, found the path to Enlightenment. It was December eighth, when the prince became a Buddha at thirty-five years of age.

6. From this time on the prince was known by different names: some spoke of him as Buddha, the Perfectly

Enlightened One, Tathagata; some spoke of him as Shakyamuni, the Sage of the Shakya clan; others called him the World-honoured One.

He went first to Mrigadava in Varanasi where the five mendicants who had lived with him during the six years of his ascetic life were staying. At first they shunned him, but after they had talked with him, they believed in him and became his first followers. He then went to the Rajagriha castle and won over King Bimbisara who had always been his friend. From there he went about the country living on alms and teaching men to accept his way of life.

Men responded to him as the thirsty seek water and the hungry food. Two great disciples, Sariputra and Maudgalyayana, and their two thousand followers, came to him.

At first the Buddha's father, king Shuddhodana, still inwardly suffering because of his son's decision to leave the place, remained aloof, but then became his faithful disciple. Mahaprajapati, the Buddha's stepmother of the Shakya clan began to follow him. Multitudes of others also became his devoted and faithful followers.

7. For forty-five years the Buddha went about the country preaching and persuading men to follow his way of life. But when he was eighty, at Vaisali and on his way from Rajagriha to Shravasti, he became ill and predicted that after three months he would enter Nirvana. Still he journeyed on until he reached Pava where he fell seriously ill from some food offered by Chunda, a blacksmith. Eventually, in spite of great pain and weakness, he reached the forest that bordered Kusinagara.

Lying between two large *sal* trees, he continued teaching his disciples until his last moment. Thus he entered into perfect tranquillity after he had completed his work as the world's greatest teacher.

8. Under the guidance of Ananda, the Buddha's favourite disciple, the body was cremated by his friends in Kusinagara.

Seven neighbouring rulers as well as King Ajatasatru demanded that the relics be divided among them. The people of Kusinagara at first refused and the dispute even threatened to end in war; but under the advice of a wise man named Drona, the crisis passed and the relics were divided among the eight great countries. The ashes of the funeral pyre and the earthen jar that contained the relics were also given to two other rulers to be likewise honoured. Thus ten great towers commemorating the Buddha were built to enshrine his relics and ashes.

II

The Last Teachings of the Buddha

1.   Beneath the *sal* trees at Kusinagara, in his last words to his disciples, the Buddha said:

"Make of yourself a light. Rely upon yourself: do not depend upon anyone else. Make my teachings your light. Rely upon them: do not depend upon any other teaching.

Consider your body: Think of its impurity. Knowing that its pain and its delight are alike − causes of suffering, how can you indulge in its desires? Consider your 'self'; think of its transiency; how can you fall into delusion about it and cherish pride and selfishness, knowing that they must all end in inevitable suffering? Consider all substances; can you find among them any enduring 'self'? Are they not all aggregates that sooner or later will break apart and be scattered? Do not be confused by the universality of suffering, but follow my teaching, even after my death, and you will be rid of pain. Do this and you will indeed be my disciples."

2.   "My disciples, the teachings that I have given you are never to be forgotten or abandoned. They are always to be treasured, they are to be thought about, they are to be practised. If you follow these teachings you will always be happy.

"The point of the teachings is to control your own mind. Keep your mind from greed, and you will keep your behaviour right, your mind pure and your words faithful. By always thinking about the transiency of your life, you will be able to resist greed and anger, and will be able to avoid all evils.

"If you find your mind tempted and so entangled in greed, you must suppress and control the temptation; be the master of your own mind.

"A man's mind may make him a Buddha, or it may make him a beast. Misled by error, one becomes a demon; enlightened, one becomes a Buddha. Therefore, control your mind and do not let it deviate from the right path."

3. "You should respect each other, follow my teachings, and refrain from disputes; you should not, like water and oil, repel each other, but should, like milk and water, mingle together.

"Study together, learn together, practise my teachings together. Do not waste your mind and time in idleness and quarrelling. Enjoy the blossoms of Enlightenment in their season and harvest the fruit of the right path.

"If you neglect them, it means that you have never really met me. It means that you are far from me, even if you are actually with me; but if you accept and practise my teachings, then you are very near to me, even though you are far away."

4. "My disciples, my end is approaching, our parting is near, but do not lament. Life is ever changing; none can escape the dissolution of the body. This I am now to show by my own death, my body falling apart like a dilapidated cart.

"Do not vainly lament, but realise that nothing is permanent and learn from it the emptiness of human life. Do not cherish the unworthy desire that the changeable might become unchanging.

"The demon of worldly desires is always seeking chances to deceive the mind. If a viper lives in your room and you wish to have a peaceful sleep, you must first chase it out.

"You must break the bonds of worldly passions and drive them away as you would a viper. You must positively protect your own mind."

5. "My disciples, my last moment has come, but do not forget that death is only the end of the physical body. The body was born from parents and was nourished by food; just as inevitable are sickness and death.

"But the true Buddha is not a human body: – it is Enlightenment. A human body must die, but the Wisdom of Enlightenment will exist forever in the truth of the Dharma, and in the practice of the Dharma. He who sees merely my body does not truly see me. Only he who accepts my teachings truly sees me.

"After my death, the Dharma shall be your teacher. Follow the Dharma and you will be true to me.

"During the last forty-five years of my life, I have withheld nothing from my teachings. There is no secret teaching, no hidden meaning; everything has been taught openly and clearly. My dear disciples, this is the end. In a moment, I shall be passing into Nirvana. This is my instruction."

Chapter Two

The Eternal and Glorified Buddha

I

His Compassion and Vows

1. The Spirit of Buddha is that of great loving kindness and compassion. The great loving kindness is the spirit to save all people by any and all means. The great compassion is the spirit that prompts it to be ill with the illness of people, to suffer with their sufferings.

"Your suffering is my suffering and your happiness is my happiness," said Buddha, and, just as a mother always loves her child, He does not forget that spirit even for a single moment, for it is the nature of Buddhahood to be compassionate.

The Buddha's spirit of compassion is stimulated according to the needs of men; man's faith is the reaction to this spirit, and it leads him to Enlightenment, just as a mother realises her motherhood by loving her child; then the child, reacting to that love, feels safe and at ease.

Yet people do not understand this spirit of Buddha and go on suffering from the illusions and desires that arise from their ignorance; they suffer from their own deeds accumulated through worldly passions, and wander about among the mountains of delusion with the heavy burden of their evil deeds.

2. Do not think that the compassion of the Buddha is only for the present life; it is a manifestation of the timeless compassion of the eternal Buddha that has been operative since unknown time, when mankind went astray due to ignorance.

The eternal Buddha always appears before people in the most friendly forms and brings to them the wisest methods of relief.

Shakyamuni Buddha, born a prince among his Shakya kinsmen, left the comforts of his home to live a life of asceticism. Through the practice of silent meditation, he realised Enlightenment. He preached the Dharma (the teaching) among his fellow-men and finally manifested it by his earthly death.

The working of Buddhahood is as everlasting as human ignorance is endless; and as the depth of ignorance is bottomless, so Buddha's compassion is boundless.

When Buddha decided to break from the worldly life, he made four great vows: 1) To save all people; 2) To renounce all worldly desires; 3) To learn all the teachings; and 4) To attain perfect Enlightenment. These vows were manifestations of the love and compassion that are fundamental to the nature of Buddhahood.

3. Buddha first taught himself to avoid the sin of killing any living creature, he wished that all people might know the blessedness of a long life.

Buddha trained himself to avoid the sin of stealing, he wished that all people might have everything they needed.

Buddha trained himself to avoid ever committing adultery, he wished that all people might know the blessedness of a pure spirit and not suffer from insatiable desires.

Buddha, aiming at his ideal, trained himself to remain free from all deception, he wished that all people might know the tranquillity of mind that would follow in speaking the truth.

He trained himself to avoid double-talk, he wished that all people might know the joy of fellowship.

He trained himself to avoid abusing others, and then he wished that all might have the serene mind that would follow by living in peace with others.

He kept himself free from idle talk, and then wished that all might know the blessedness of sympathetic understanding.

Buddha, aiming at his ideal, trained himself to keep free from greed, and by this virtuous deed he wished that all people might know the peacefulness that would go with this freedom.

He trained himself to avoid anger, and he wished that all people might love one another.

He trained himself to avoid ignorance, and he wished that all people might understand and not disregard the law of causation.

Thus Buddha's compassion embraces all people, and his constant consideration is for their happiness. He loves people as parents love their children and he wishes the highest blessedness for them, namely, that they will be able to pass beyond this ocean of life and death.

II

Buddha's Relief and Salvation for Us

1. It is very difficult for the words spoken by Buddha from the far bank of Enlightenment to reach the people still struggling in the world of delusion; therefore Buddha returns to this world Himself and uses His methods of salvation.

"Now I will tell you a parable," Buddha said, "Once there lived a wealthy man whose house caught fire. The man was away from home and when he came back, he found that his children were so absorbed in playing that they had not noticed the fire and were still inside the house. The father screamed, 'Get out, children! Come out of the house! Hurry!' But the children did not heed him.

"The anxious father shouted again. 'Children, I have some wonderful toys here; come out of the house and get them!' Heeding his cry this time, the children ran out of the burning house."

This world is a burning house. The people, unaware that the house is on fire, are in danger of being burned to death so Buddha in compassion devises ways of saving them.

2. Buddha said: "I will tell you another parable. Once upon a time the only son of a wealthy man left his home and fell into extreme poverty.

"When the father travelled far from home in search of his son, he lost track of him. He did everything he could to find his son, but in vain.

"Decades later, his son, now reduced to wretchedness, wandered near where his father was living.

"The father quickly recognised his son and sent his servants to bring the wanderer home; who was overcome by the majestic appearance of the mansion. He feared that they were deceiving him and would not go with them. He did not realise it was his own father.

"The father again sent his servants to offer him some money to become a servant in their rich master's household. The son accepted the offer and returned with them to his father's house and became a servant.

"The father gradually advanced him until he was put in charge of all the property and treasures, but still the son did not recognise his own father.

"The father was pleased with his son's faithfulness, and as the end of his life drew near, he called together his relatives and friends and told them: 'Friends, this is my only son, the son I sought for many years. From now on, all my property and treasures belong to him.'

"The son was surprised at his father's confession and said: 'Not only have I found my father but all this property and treasure is now mine.'"

The wealthy man in this parable represents Buddha, and the wandering son, all people. Buddha's compassion embraces all people with the love of a father for his only son. In that love he conceives the wisest methods to lead, teach and enrich them with the treasure of Enlightenment.

3. Just as rain falls on all vegetation, so Buddha's compassion extends equally to all people. Just as different plants receive particular benefits from the same rain, so people of different natures and circumstances are blessed in different ways.

4. Parents love all their children, but their love is expressed with special care toward those who, because of their ignorance, have heavier burdens of evil and suffering to bear.

The sun rises in the eastern sky and clears away the darkness of the world without prejudice or favouritism toward any particular region. So Buddha's compassion encompasses all people, encouraging them to do right and guides them against evil. Thus, He clears away the darkness of ignorance and leads people to Enlightenment.

Buddha is a father in His compassion and a mother in His loving kindness. In their ignorance and bondage to worldly desire, people often act with excessive zeal. Buddha is also zealous, but out of compassion for all people. They are helpless without Buddha's compassion and must receive His methods of salvation as His children.

III

The Eternal Buddha

1. Common people believe that Buddha was born a prince and learned the way to Enlightenment as a mendicant; actually, Buddha has always existed in the world which is without beginning or end.

As the Eternal Buddha, He has known all people and applied all methods of relief.

There is no falsity in the Eternal Dharma which Buddha taught, for He knows all things in the world as they are, and He teaches them to all people.

Indeed, it is very difficult to understand the world as it is, for, although it seems true, it is not, and, although it seems false, it is not. Ignorant people can not know the truth concerning the world.

Buddha alone truly and fully knows the world as it is and He never says that it is true or false, or good or evil. He simply portrays the world as it is.

What Buddha does teach is this: "That all people should cultivate roots of virtue according to their natures, their deeds, and their beliefs." This teaching transcends all affirmation and negation of this world.

2. Buddha teaches not only through words, but also through His life. Although His life is endless, in order to awaken greedy people, He uses the expedient of death.

"While a certain physician was away from home, his children accidentally took some poison. When the physician returned, he noticed their sickness and prepared an antidote. Some of the children who were not seriously poisoned accepted the medicine and were cured, but others were so seriously affected that they refused to take the medicine.

The physician, prompted by his paternal love for his children, decided on an extreme method to press the cure upon them. He said to the children: 'I must go off on a long journey. I am old and may pass away any day. If I am with you I can care for you, but If I should pass away, you will become worse and worse. If you hear of my death, I implore you to take the antidote and be cured of this subtle poisoning.' Then he went on the long journey. After a time, he sent a messenger to his children to inform them of his death."

The children, receiving the message, were deeply affected by the thought of their father's death and by the realization that they would no longer have the benefit of his benevolent care. Recalling his parting request, in a feeling of sorrow and helplessness, took the medicine and recovered.

People must not condemn the deception of this father-physician. Buddha is like that father. He, too, employs the fiction of life and death to save people who are entangled in the bondage of desires.

Chapter Three

The Form of Buddha and His Virtues

I

Three Aspects of Buddha's Body

1. Do not seek to know Buddha by His form or attributes; for neither the form nor the attributes are the real Buddha. The true Buddha is Enlightenment itself. The true way to know Buddha is to realise Enlightenment.

If someone sees some excellent features of Buddha and then thinks he knows Buddha, his is the mistake of an ignorant eye, for the true Buddha can not be embodied in a form or seen by human eyes. Neither can one know Buddha by a faultless description of his attributes. It is not possible to describe His attributes in human words.

Though we speak of His form, the Eternal Buddha has no set form, but can manifest Himself in any form. Though we describe His attributes, yet the Eternal Buddha has no set attributes, but can manifest Himself in any and all excellent attributes.

So, if one sees distinctly the form of Buddha, or perceives His attributes clearly, and yet does not become attached to His form or to His attributes, he has the capacity to see and know Buddha.

2. Buddha's body is Enlightenment itself. Being formless and without substance, it always has been and always will be. It is

not a physical body that must be nourished by food. It is an
eternal body whose substance is Wisdom. Buddha, therefore,
has neither fear nor disease; He is eternally changeless.

Therefore, Buddha will never disappear as long as
Enlightenment exists. Enlightenment appears as the light of
wisdom that awakens people into a newness of life and causes
them to be born into the world of Buddha.

Those who realise this become the children of Buddha;
they keep His Dharma, honour His teachings and pass them
on to posterity. Nothing can be more miraculous than the
power of Buddha.

3.   Buddha has a threefold body. There is an aspect of Essence
or Dharma-kaya; there is an aspect of Potentiality or
Sambhoga-kaya; and there is an aspect of Manifestation or
Nirmana-kaya.

Dharma-kaya is the substance of the Dharma; that is, it is
the substance of Truth itself. In the aspect of Essence, Buddha
has no shape or colour, and since Buddha has no shape or
colour, He comes from nowhere and there is nowhere for Him
to go. Like the blue sky, He arches over everything, and since
He is all things, He lacks nothing.

He does not exist because people think He exists; neither
does He disappear because people forget Him. He is under no
particular compulsion to appear when people are happy and
comfortable, neither is it necessary for Him to disappear when
people are inattentive and idle. Buddha transcends every
conceivable direction of human thought.

Buddha's body in this aspect fills every corner of the
universe; it reaches everywhere, it exists forever, regardless of
whether people believe in Him or doubt His existence.

4.   Sambhoga-kaya signifies that the nature of Buddha, the
merging of both Compassion and Wisdom, which is imageless
spirit, manifests itself through the symbols of birth and death,
through the symbols of vow-making, training and revealing
His sacred name, in order to lead all people to salvation.

Compassion is the Essence of this body and in its spirit Buddha uses all devices to emancipate all those who are ready for emancipation. Like a fire that, once kindled, never dies until the fuel is exhausted, so the Compassion of Buddha will never falter until all worldly passions are exhausted. Just as the wind blows away the dust, so the Compassion of Buddha in this body blows away the dust of human suffering.

Nirmana-kaya signifies that, in order to complete the relief of Buddha of Potentiality, Buddha appeared in the world in bodily form and showed the people, according to their natures and capacities, the aspects of the birth, renunciation of this world and attainment of Enlightenment. In order to lead the people, Buddha in this body uses every means such as illness and death.

The form of Buddha is originally one Dharma-kaya, but as the nature of people varies, Buddha's form appears differently. Although the form of Buddha varies according to the different desires, deeds and abilities of people, Buddha is concerned only with the truth of the Dharma.

Though Buddha has a threefold body, His spirit and purpose are one – to save all people.

In all circumstances Buddha is manifest in His purity, yet manifestation is not Buddha because Buddha is not a form. Buddhahood fills everything; it makes Enlightenment its body and, as Enlightenment, it appears before all those capable of realizing the Truth.

II

The Appearance of Buddha

1. It is seldom that a Buddha appears in this world. Now a Buddha does appear, attains Enlightenment, introduces the Dharma, severs the net of suspicion, removes the lure of desire at its root, plugs the fountain of evil. Completely unhindered He walks at will over the world. There is nothing greater than to revere the Buddha.

Buddha appears in the world of suffering because He can not desert suffering people. His only purpose is to spread the Dharma and to bless all people with its Truth.

It is very difficult to introduce the Dharma into a world filled with injustice and false standards, a world that is vainly struggling with insatiable desires and discomforts. Buddha faces these difficulties because of His great love and compassion.

2. Buddha is a good friend to all people. If Buddha finds a man suffering from the heavy burden of worldly passions. He feels compassion and shares the burden with him. If He meets a man suffering from delusion, He will clear away the delusion by pure light of His wisdom.

Like a calf which enjoys its life with its mother, those who have heard the Buddha's teachings are afterward unwilling to leave Him because His teachings bring them happiness.

3. When the moon sets, people say that the moon has disappeared; and when the moon rises, they say that the moon has appeared. In fact, the moon neither goes nor comes, but shines continually in the sky. Buddha is exactly like the moon: He neither appears nor disappears; He only seems to do so out of love for the people that He may teach them.

People call one phase of the moon a full moon, they call another phase a crescent moon; in reality, the moon is always perfectly round, neither waxing nor waning. Buddha is precisely like the moon. In the eyes of men, Buddha may seem to change in appearance, but, in truth, Buddha does not change.

The moon appears everywhere, over a crowded city, a sleepy village, a mountain, a river. It is seen in the depths of a pond, in a jug of water, in a drop of dew hanging on a leaf. If a man walks hundreds of miles the moon goes with him. To men the moon seems to change, but the moon does not change. Buddha is like the moon in following the people of this world in all their changing circumstances, manifesting various appearances; but in His Essence He does not change.

4. The fact that Buddha appears and disappears can be explained by causality: namely, when the cause and conditions are propitious, Buddha appears; when causes and conditions are not propitious, Buddha seems to disappear from the world.

Whether Buddha appears or disappears, Buddhahood always remains the same. Knowing this principle, one must keep to the path of Enlightenment and attain Perfect Wisdom, undisturbed by the apparent changes in the image of Buddha, in the condition of the world, or in the fluctuations of human thought.

It has been explained that Buddha is not a physical body but is Enlightenment. A body may be thought of as a receptacle; then, if this receptacle is filled with Enlightenment, it may be called Buddha. Therefore, if anyone is attached to the physical body of Buddha and laments His disappearance, he will be unable to see the true Buddha.

In reality, the true nature of all things transcends the discrimination of appearance and disappearance, of coming and going, of good and evil. All things are substanceless and perfectly homogeneous.

Such discrimination are caused by an erroneous judgement by those who see phenomena. The true form of Buddha neither appears nor disappears.

III

Buddha's Virtue

1. Buddha receives the respect of the world because of five virtues: superior conduct; superior point of view; perfect wisdom; superior preaching ability; and the power to lead people to the practice of His teachings.

In addition, eight other virtues enable Buddha to bestow blessings and happiness upon the people: the ability to bring immediate benefits in the world through the practice of His teachings, the ability to judge correctly lead people to Enlightenment by teaching the right way, the ability to lead all people by an equal way, the ability to avoid pride and boasting, the ability to do what He has spoken, the ability to say what He has done, and, thus doing, to fulfil the vows of His compassionate heart.

Through meditation, Buddha preserves a calm and peaceful spirit, radiant with mercy, compassion, happiness and even equanimity. He deals equitably with all people, cleansing their minds of defilement and bestowing happiness in a perfect singleness of spirit.

2. Buddha is both father and mother to the people of the world. For sixteen months after a child is born the father and mother have to speak to him in babyish words; then gradually they teach him to speak as an adult. Like earthly parents, Buddha first takes care of the people and then leaves them to care for themselves. He first brings things to pass according to their desires and then He brings them to a peaceful and safe shelter.

What Buddha preaches in His language, people receive and assimilate in their own language as if it were intended exclusively for them.

Buddha's state of mind surpasses human thought; it cannot be made clear by words; it can only be hinted at in parables.

The Ganges River is stirred up by the tramping of horses and elephants and disturbed by the movements of fish and turtles; but the river flows on, pure and undisturbed by such trifles. Buddha is like the great river. The fish and turtles of other teachings swim about in its depths and push against its current, but in vain. Buddha's Dharma flows on, pure and undisturbed.

3. Buddha's Wisdom, being perfect, keeps away from extremes of prejudice and preserves a moderation that is beyond all words to describe. Being all-wise He knows the

thoughts and feelings of all men and realises everything in this world in a moment.

As the stars of heaven are reflected in the calm sea, so people's thought, feelings and circumstances are reflected in the depths of Buddha's Wisdom. This is why Buddha is called the Perfectly Enlightened One, the Omniscience.

Buddha's Wisdom refreshes the arid minds of people, enlightens them and teaches them the significance of this world, its causes and its effects, appearings and disappearings. Indeed, without the aid of Buddha's Wisdom, what aspect of the world is at all comprehensible for people?

4.   Buddha does not always appear as a Buddha. Sometimes He appears as an incarnation of evil, sometimes as a woman, a god, a king, or a statesman; sometimes He appears in a brothel or in a gambling house.

In an epidemic He appears as a healing physician and in war He preaches forbearance and mercy for the suffering people; for those who believe that things are everlasting, He preaches transiency and uncertainty; for those who are proud and egoistic, He preaches humility and self-sacrifice; for those who are misery of the world.

The work of Buddha is to manifest in all affairs and on all occasions the pure essence of Dharma-kaya (the absolute nature of Buddha); so Buddha's mercy and compassion flow out from this Dharma-kaya in endless life and boundless light, bringing salvation to mankind.

5.   The world is like a burning house that is forever being destroyed and rebuilt. People, being confused by the darkness of the ignorance, lose their minds in anger, displeasure, jealousy, prejudice and worldly passion. They are like babies in need of a mother; everyone must be dependent upon Buddha's mercy and compassion.

Buddha is a father to all the world; all human beings are the children of Buddha. Buddha is the most saintly of saints. The world is afire with decrepitude and death; there is

suffering everywhere. But people, engrossed in the vain search
for worldly pleasure, are not wise enough to fully realise this.

Buddha saw that world of delusion was really a burning
house, so He turned from it and found refuge and peace in the
quiet forest. There, out of His great compassion, he calls to us:
"This world of change and suffering belongs to me; all these
ignorant, heedless people are my children; I am the only one
who can save them from their delusion and misery."

As Buddha is the great king of the Dharma, He can preach
to all people as He wishes. Buddha appears in the world to
bless the people. To save them from suffering He preaches the
Dharma, but the ears of people are dulled by greed and they
are inattentive.

But those who listen to His teachings are free from the
delusions and the miseries of life. "People cannot be saved by
relying on their own wisdom," He said, "and through faith they
must enter into my teaching." Therefore, one should listen to
the Buddha's teachings and put it into practice.

Part – II
DHARMA

Chapter One

Causation

I

The Fourfold Noble Truth

1. The world is full of suffering. Birth is suffering, old age is suffering, sickness and death are sufferings. To meet a man whom one hates is suffering, to be separated from a beloved one is suffering, to be vainly struggling to satisfy one's needs is suffering. In fact, life that is not free from desire and passion is always involved with distress. This is called the Truth of Suffering.

The cause of human suffering is undoubtedly found in the thirsts of the physical body and in the illusions of wordily passion. If these thirsts and illusions are traced to their source, they are found to be rooted in the intense desires of physical instincts. Thus, desire, having a strong will-to-live as its basis, seeks that which it feels desirable, even if it is sometimes death. This is called the Truth of the Cause of Suffering.

If desire, which lies at the root of all human passion, can be removed, the passion will die out and all human suffering will be ended. This is called the Truth of the Cessation of Suffering.

In order to enter into a state where there is no desire and no suffering, one must follow a certain Path. The stages of this Noble Eightfold Path are: Right View, Right Thought, Right Speech, Right Behaviour, Right Livelihood, Right Effort, Right Mindfulness and Right Concentration. This is called the Truth of the Noble Path to the Cessation of the Cause of Suffering.

People should keep these Truths clearly in mind, for the world is filled with suffering and if anyone wishes to escape from suffering, he must sever the ties of worldly passion which is the sole cause of suffering. The way of life which is free from worldly passion and suffering can only be known through Enlightenment, and Enlightenment can only be attained through the discipline of the Noble Eightfold Path.

2.   All those who are seeking Enlightenment must understand the Fourfold Noble Truth. Without understanding this, they will wander about interminably in the bewildering maze of life's illusions. Those who understand this Fourfold Noble Truth are called "the people who have acquired the eyes of Enlightenment."

Therefore, those who wish to follow the Buddha's teachings should concentrate their minds on this Fourfold Noble Truth and seek to make their understanding of its meaning clear. In all ages, a saint, if he is a true saint, is one who understands it and teaches it to others.

When a man clearly understands the Fourfold Noble Truth, then the Noble Eightfold Path will lead him away from greed; and if he is free from greed, he will not quarrel with the world, he will not kill, nor steal, nor commit adultery, nor cheat, nor abuse, nor flatter, nor envy, nor lose his temper, nor forget the transiency of life nor will he be unjust.

3.   Following the Noble Path is like entering a dark room with a light in the hand: the darkness will all be cleared away and the room will be filled with light.

People who understand the meaning of the Noble Truths and have learned to follow the Noble Path are in possession of the light of wisdom that will clear away the darkness of ignorance.

Buddha leads people, merely by indicating to them the Fourfold Noble Truth. Those who understand it properly will attain Enlightenment; they will be able to guide and support others in this bewildering world, and they will be worthy of trust. When the Fourfold Noble Truth is clearly understood, all the sources of worldly passion are dried up.

Advancing from this Fourfold Noble Truth, the disciples of Buddha will attain all other precious truths; they will gain the wisdom and insight to understand all meanings, and will become capable of preaching the Dharma to all the peoples of the world.

II

Causation

1. There are causes for all human suffering, and there is a way by which they may be ended, because everything in the world is the result of a vast concurrence of causes and conditions, and everything disappears as these causes and conditions change and pass away.

Rain falls, winds blow, plants bloom, leaves mature and are blown away. These phenomena are all interrelated with causes and conditions, and are brought about by them, and disappear as the causes and conditions change.

One is born through the conditions of parentage. His body is nourished by food: his spirit is nurtured by teaching and experience.

Therefore, both flesh and spirit are related to conditions and are changed as conditions change.

As a net is made up by a series of knots, so everything in this world is connected by a series of knots. If anyone thinks that the mesh of a net is an independent, isolated thing, he is mistaken.

It is called a net because it is made up of a series of connected meshes, and each mesh has its place and responsibilities in relation to other meshes.

2. Blossoms come about because of a series of conditions that lead up to their blooming. Leaves are blown away because a series of conditions lead up to it. Blossoms do not appear independently, nor does leaf fall of itself, out of its season. So

everything has its coming forth and passing away; nothing can be independent without any change.

It is everlasting and unchanging rule of this world that everything is created by a series of causes and conditions and everything disappears by the same rule; everything changes, nothing remains constant.

III

Dependent Origination

1. Where is the source of human grief, lamentation, pain and agony? Is it not to be found in the fact that people are generally desirous.

They cling obstinately to lives of wealth and honour, comfort and pleasure, excitement and self-indulgence, ignorant of the fact that the desire for these very things is the source of human suffering.

From its beginning, the world has been filled with a succession of calamities, over and above the unavoidable facts of illness, old age and death.

But if one carefully considers all the facts, one must be convinced that at the basis of all suffering lies the principle of craving desire. If avarice can be removed, human suffering will come to an end.

Ignorance is manifested in greed that fills the human mind.

It comes from the fact that men are unaware of the true reason for the succession of things.

From ignorance and greed there spring impure desires for things that are, in fact, unobtainable, but for which men restlessly and blindly search.

Because of ignorance and greed, people imagine discriminations where, in reality, there are no discriminations. Inherently, there is no discrimination of right and wrong in human behaviour; but people, because of ignorance, imagine such distinctions and judge them as right or wrong.

Because of their ignorance, all people are always thinking wrong thoughts and always losing the right viewpoint and, clinging to their egos, they take wrong actions. As a result, they become attached to a delusive existence.

Making their deeds the field for their egos, using the working of discrimination of the mind as seed, beclouding the mind by ignorance, fertilising it with the rain of craving desires, irrigating it by the wilfulness of egotism, they add the conception of evil, and carry this incarnation of delusion about with them.

2. In reality, therefore, it is their own mind that causes the delusions of grief, lamentation, pain and agony.

This whole world of delusion is nothing but a shadow caused by the mind. And yet, it is also from this same mind that the world of Enlightenment appears.

3. In this world there are three wrong viewpoints. If one clings to these viewpoints, then all things in this world are but to be denied.

First, some say that all human experience is based on destiny; second, some hold that everything is created by God and controlled by His will; third, some say that everything happens by chance without having any cause or condition.

If all has been decided by destiny, both good and evil deeds are predetermined, weal and woe are predestined; nothing would exist that has not been foreordained. Then all human plans and efforts for improvement and progress would be in vain and humanity would be without hope.

The same is true of the other viewpoints, for, if everything in the last resort is in the hands of an unknowable God, or of blind chance, what hope has humanity except in submission? It is no wonder that people holding these conceptions lose hope and neglect efforts to act wisely and to avoid evil.

In fact, these three conceptions or viewpoints are all wrong: everything is a succession of appearances whose source is the accumulation of causes and conditions.

Chapter Two

The Theory of Mind-Only and the Real State of Things

I

Impermanency and Egolessness

1. Though both body and mind appear because of cooperating causes, it does not follow that there is an ego-personality. As the body of flesh is an aggregate of elements, it is, therefore, impermanent.

If the body were an ego-personality, it could do this and that as it would determine.

A king has the power to praise or punish as he wishes, but he becomes ill despite his intent or desire, he comes to old age unwillingly, and his fortune and his wishes often have little to do with each other.

Neither is the mind the ego-personality. The human mind is an aggregate of causes and conditions. It is in constant change.

If the mind were an ego-personality, it could do this and that as it would determine; but the mind often flies from what it knows is right and chases after evil reluctantly. Still, nothing seems to happen exactly as its ego desires.

2. If one is asked whether the body is constant or impermanent, he will be obliged to answer "impermanent".

If one is asked whether impermanent existence is happiness or suffering, he will generally have to answer "suffering".

If a man believes that such an impermanent thing, so changeable and filled with suffering, is the ego-personality, it is a serious mistake.

The human mind is also impermanent and suffering; it has nothing that can be called an ego-personality.

Our true body and mind, which make up an individual life, and the external world surrounding it, are far apart from both the conceptions of "me" and "mine".

It is simply the mind clouded over by impure desires, and impervious to wisdom, that obstinately persists in thinking of "me" and "mine".

Since both body and its surroundings are originated by cooperating causes and conditions, they are continually changing and never can come to an end.

The human mind, in its never-ending changes, is like the flowing water of river or the burning flame of a candle; like an ape, it is forever jumping about, not ceasing for even a moment.

A wise man, seeing and hearing such, should break away from any attachment to body or mind, if he is ever to attain Enlightenment.

3.   There are five things which no one is able to accomplish in this world: first, to cease growing old when he is growing old; second, to cease being sick; third, to cease dying; fourth, to deny extinction when there is extinction; fifth, to deny exhaustion.

Ordinary people in the world sooner or later run into these facts, and most people suffer consequently, but those who have heard the Buddha's teachings do not suffer because they understand that these are unavoidable.

There are four truths in this world: first, all living beings rise from ignorance; second, all objects of desire are impermanent, uncertain and suffering; third, all existing things are also impermanent, uncertain and suffering; fourth, there is nothing that can be called an "ego", and there is no such thing as "mine" in all the world.

These truths that everything is impermanent and passing
and egoless, have no connection with the fact of Buddha's
appearing or not appearing in this world. These truths are
certain; Buddha knows this and, therefore, preaches the
Dharma to all people.

II

The Theory of Mind-Only

1. Both delusion and Enlightenment originate within the
mind, and every existence or phenomenon arises from the
functions of the mind, just as different things appear from the
sleeve of a magician.

The activities of the mind have no limit, they form the
surroundings of life. An impure mind surrounds itself with
impure things and a pure mind surrounds itself with pure
things; hence, surroundings have no more limits than the
activities of the mind.

Just as a picture is drawn by an artist, surroundings are
created by the activities of the mind. While the surroundings
created by Buddha are pure and free from defilement, those
created by ordinary men are not so.

The mind conjures up multifarious forms just as a skilful
painter creates pictures of various worlds. There is nothing in
the world that is not mind-created. A Buddha is like our mind;
sentient beings are just like Buddhas. Therefore there is no
difference among the mind, Buddhas and sentient beings in
their capability of creating all things.

Buddha has a right understanding of all things as fashioned
by the moral mind. Therefore, those who know this are able to
see the real Buddha.

2. But the mind that creates its surroundings is never free
from memories, fears or laments, not only in the past but in the
present and the future, because they have arisen from
ignorance and greed.

It is from ignorance and greed that the world of delusion is born, and all the vast complexity of coordinating causes and conditions exists within the mind and nowhere else.

Both life and death arise from the mind and exist within the mind. Hence, when the mind that concerns itself with life and death passes on, the world of life and death passes with it.

An unenlightened life rises from a mind that is bewildered by its own world of delusion. If we learn that there is no world of delusion outside the mind, the bewildered mind becomes clear; and because we cease to create impure surroundings, we attain Enlightenment.

In this way the world of life and death is created by the mind, is in bondage to the mind, is ruled by the mind; the mind is the master of every situation. The world of suffering is brought about by the deluded mortal mind.

3.   Therefore, all things are primarily controlled and ruled by the mind, and are created up by the mind. As the wheels follow the ox that draws the cart, so does suffering follow the person who speaks and acts with an impure mind.

But if a man speaks and acts with a good mind, happiness follows him like his shadow. Those who act evil are followed by the thought, "I have done wrong." And the memory of the act is stored to work out its inevitable retribution in the lives to follow. But those who act with good motives are made happy by the thought, "I have done good," and are made happier by the thought that the good act will bring continuing happiness in the lives to follow.

If the mind is impure, it will cause the feet to stumble along a rough and difficult road; there will be many a fall and much pain. But if the mind is pure, the path will be smooth and the journey peaceful.

One who is to enjoy the purity of both body and mind walks the path to Buddhahood, breaking the net of selfish, impure thoughts and evil desires. He who is calm in mind acquires peacefulness and thus is able to cultivate his mind day and night with more diligence.

III

Real State of Things

1. Since everything in this world is brought about by causes and conditions, there can be no fundamental distinctions among things. The apparent distinctions exist because of people's absurd and discriminating thoughts.

In the sky there is no distinction of east and west; people create the distinctions out of their own minds and then believe them to be true.

Mathematical numbers from one to infinity are each complete numbers, and each in itself carries no distinction of quantity; but people make the discrimination for their own convenience, so as to be able to indicate varying amounts.

Inherently there are no distinctions between the process of life and the process of destruction; people make a discrimination and call one birth and the other death. In action there is no discrimination between right and wrong, but people make a distinction for their own convenience.

Buddha keeps away from these discriminations and looks upon the world as upon a passing cloud. To Buddha every definitive thing is illusion; He knows that whatever the mind grasps and throws away is insubstantial; thus He transcends the pitfalls of images and discriminative thought.

2. People grasp at things for their own imagined convenience and comfort; they grasp at wealth and treasure and honours; they cling desperately to mortal life.

They make arbitrary distinctions between existence and nonexistence, good and bad, right and wrong. For people, life is a succession of graspings and attachments, and then, because of this, they must assume the illusions of pain and suffering.

Once there was a man on a long journey who came to a river. He said to himself: "This side of the river is very difficult and dangerous to walk on, and the other side seems easier and safer, but how shall I get across?" So he built a raft out of branches and reeds and safely crossed the river. Then he thought to himself: 'This raft has been very useful to me in crossing the river; I will not abandon it to rot on the bank, but will carry it along with me.' And thus he voluntarily assumed an unnecessary burden. Can this man be called a wise man?

This parable teaches that even a good thing, when it becomes an unnecessary burden, should be thrown away; much more so if it is a bad thing. Buddha made it the rule of his life to avoid useless and unnecessary discussions.

3. Things do not come and go; neither do they appear and disappear; therefore, one does not get things or lose things.

Buddha teaches that things neither appear nor disappear since they transcend both the affirmation of existence and the denial of existence. That is, everything being a concordance and succession of causes and conditions, a thing in itself does not exist, so it can be said that it is nonexistent. At the same time, because it has a relative connection with causes and conditions, it can be said that it is not nonexistent.

To adhere to a thing because of its form is the source of delusion. If the form is not grasped and adhered to, this false imagination and absurd delusion will not occur. Enlightenment is seeing this truth and being free from such a foolish delusion.

The world, indeed, is like a dream and the treasures of the world are an alluring mirage. Like the apparent distances in a picture, things have no reality in themselves but are like heat haze.

4. To believe that things created by an incalculable series of causes can last forever is a serious mistake and is called the theory of permanency; but it is just as great a mistake to believe that things completely disappear; this is called the theory of nonexistence.

These categories of everlasting life and death, and existence and nonexistence, do not apply to the essential nature of things, but only to their appearances as they are observed by defiled human eyes. Because of human desire, people become related and attached to these appearances; but in the essential nature of things, they are free from all such discriminations and attachments.

Since everything is created by a series of causes and conditions, the appearances of things are constantly changing; that is, there is no consistency about it as there should be about authentic substances. It is because of this constant changing of appearances that we liken things to a mirage and a dream. But, in spite of this constant change in appearances, things, in their essential spiritual nature, are constant and changeless.

To a man a river seems like a river, but to a hungry demon which sees fire in water, it may seem to be like fire. Therefore, to speak to a man about a river existing would have some sense, but to the demon it would have no meaning.

In like manner, it can be said that things are like illusions; they can be said neither to be existent nor nonexistent.

Yet it cannot be said that, apart from this world of change and appearance, there is another world of permanence and truth. It is a mistake to regard this world as either a temporal world or as a real one.

But ignorant people of this world assume that this is a real world and proceed to act upon that absurd assumption. But as this is only an illusion, their acts, being based upon error, only lead them into harm and suffering.

A wise man, recognizing that the world is but an illusion, does not act as if it were real, so he escapes the suffering.

IV

The Middle Way

1.　To those who choose the path that leads to Enlightenment, there are two extremes that should be carefully avoided. First, there is the extreme of indulgence in the desires of the body. Second, there is the opposite extreme of ascetic discipline, torturing one's body and mind unreasonably.

The Noble Path, that transcends these two extremes and leads to Enlightenment and wisdom and peace of mind, may be called the Middle Way. What is the Middle Way? It consists of the Noble Eightfold Path: right view, right thought, right speech, right behaviour, right livelihood, right effort, right mindfulness, and right concentration.

As has been said, all things appear or disappear by reason of an endless series of causes. Ignorant people see life as either existence or nonexistence, but wise men see beyond both existence and nonexistence something that transcends them both; this is an observation of the Middle Way.

2. Suppose a log is floating in a river. If the log does not become grounded, or sink, or is not taken out by a man, or does not decay, ultimately it will reach the sea. Life is like this log caught in the current of a great river. If a person does not become attached to a life of self-indulgence, or, by renouncing life, does not become attached to a life of self-torture; if a person does not become proud of his virtues or does not become attached to his evil acts; if in his search for Enlightenment he does not become contemptuous of delusion, nor fear it, such a person is following the Middle Way.

The important thing in following the path to Enlightenment is to avoid being caught and entangled in any extreme, that is, always to follow the Middle Way.

Knowing that things neither exist nor do not exist, remembering the dream-like nature of everything, one should avoid being caught by pride of personality or praise for good deeds; or being caught and entangled by anything else.

If a person is to avoid being caught in the current of his desires, he must learn at the very beginning not to grasp at things lest he should become accustomed and attached to them. He must not become attached to existence nor to nonexistence, to anything inside or outside, neither to good things nor to bad things, neither to right nor to wrong.

If he becomes attached to things, just at that moment, all at once, the life of delusion begins. The one who follows the

Noble Path to Enlightenment will not maintain regrets, neither will he cherish anticipation, but, with an equitable and peaceful mind, will meet what comes.

3. Enlightenment has no definite form or nature by which it can manifest itself; so in Enlightenment itself, there is nothing to be enlightened.

Enlightenment exists solely because of delusion and ignorance; if they disappear, so will Enlightenment. And the opposite is true also: there is no Enlightenment apart from delusion and ignorance; no delusion and ignorance apart from Enlightenment.

Therefore, be on guard against thinking of Enlightenment as a "thing" to be grasped at, lest it, too, should become an obstruction. When the mind that was in darkness becomes enlightened, it passes away, and with its passing, the thing which we call Enlightenment also passes.

As long as people desire Enlightenment and try to grasp it, it means that delusion is still with them; therefore, those who are following the way to Enlightenment must not try to grasp it, and if they reach Enlightenment they must not linger in it.

When people attain Enlightenment in this sense, it means that everything is Enlightenment itself as it is; therefore, people should follow the path to Enlightenment until in their thoughts, worldly passions and Enlightenment become identical as they are.

4. This concept of universal oneness – that things in their essential nature have no distinguishing marks – is called "Śūnyatā." Śūnyatā means non-substantiality, the unborn, having no self-nature, no duality. It is because things in themselves have no form or characteristics that we can speak of them as neither being born nor being destroyed. There is nothing about the essential nature of things that can be described in terms of discrimination; that is why things are called non-substantial.

As has been pointed out, all things appear and disappear because of causes and conditions. Nothing ever exists entirely alone; everything is in relation to everything else.

Wherever there is light, there is shadow; wherever there is length, there is shortness; wherever there is white, there is black. Just like these, as the self-nature of things cannot exist alone, they are called non-substantial.

By the same reasoning, Enlightenment cannot exist apart from ignorance, nor ignorance apart from Enlightenment. Since things do not differ in their essential nature, there can be no duality.

5. People habitually think of themselves as being connected with birth and death, but in reality there are no such conceptions.

When people are able to realise this truth, they have realised the truth of the non-duality of birth and death.

It is because people cherish the idea of an 'ego personality' that they cling to the idea of possession; but since there is no such thing as an "ego", there can be no such things as possessions. When people are able to realise this truth, they will be able to realise the truth of "non-duality".

People cherish the distinction of purity and impurity; but in the nature of things, there is no such distinction, except as it rises from false and absurd images in their mind.

In like manner people make a distinction between good and evil, but good and evil do not exist separately. Those who are following the path to Enlightenment recognise no such duality, and it leads them to neither praise the good and condemn the evil, nor despise the good and condone the evil.

People naturally fear misfortune and long for good fortune; but if the distinction is carefully studied, misfortune often turns out to be good fortune and good fortune to be misfortune. The wise man learns to meet the changing circumstances of life with an equitable spirit, being neither elated by success nor depressed by failure. Thus one realises the truth of non-duality.

Therefore, all the words that express relations of duality – such as existence and nonexistence, worldly passions and true-knowledge, purity and impurity, good and evil – none of these terms of contrast in one's thinking are expressed or recognised in their true nature. When people keep free from such terms and from the emotions engendered by them, they realise Śūnyatā's universal truth.

6. Just as the pure and fragrant lotus flower grows out of the mud of a swamp rather than out of the clean loam of an upland field, so from the muck of worldly passions springs the pure Enlightenment of Buddhahood. Even the mistaken views of heretics and the delusions of worldly passions may be the seeds for Buddhahood.

If a diver is to secure pearls he must descend to the bottom of the sea, braving all dangers of jagged coral and vicious sharks. So man must face the perils of worldly passion if he is to secure the precious pearl of Enlightenment. He must first be lost among the mountainous crags of egoism and selfishness, before there will awaken in him the desire to find a path that will lead him to Enlightenment.

There is a legend of a hermit who had such a great desire to find the true path that he climbed a mountain of swords and threw himself into fire, enduring them because of his hope. He who is willing to risk the perils of the path will find a cool breeze blowing on the sword-bristling mountains of selfishness and among the fires of hatred, and in the end, will come to realise that the selfishness and worldly passions against which he has struggled and suffered are Enlightenment itself.

7. Buddha's teachings leads us to non-duality, from the discriminating concept of two conflicting points of view. It is a mistake for people to seek a thing supposed to be good and right, and to flee from another supposed to be bad and evil.

If people insist that all things are empty and transitory, it is just as great a mistake to insist that all things are real and do not change. If a person becomes attached to his ego, it is a mistake because it cannot save him from dissatisfaction or suffering. If he believes there is no ego, it is also a mistake and it would be useless for him to practise the Way of Truth. If people assert that everything is suffering, it is also a mistake; if they assert that everything is happiness, that is a mistake, too, Buddha teaches the Middle Way transcending these prejudiced concepts, where duality merges into oneness.

Chapter Three
Buddha-Nature

I
The Mind of Purity

1. Among humans there are many kinds and degrees of mentality: some are wise, some are foolish, some are good-natured, some are bad-tempered, some are easily led, some are difficult to lead, some possess pure minds and some have minds that are defiled; but these differences are negligible when it comes to the attainment of Enlightenment. The world is like a lotus pond filled with many varieties of the plant; there are blossoms of many different tints. Some are white, some pink, some blue, some yellow; some grow under water, some spread their leaves on the water, and some raise their leaves above the water. Mankind has many more differences. There is the difference of sex, but it is not an essential difference, for, with proper training, both men and women may attain Enlightenment.

To be a trainer of elephants, one must possess five qualifications: good health, confidence, diligence, sincerity of purpose, and wisdom. To follow the Buddha's Noble Path to Enlightenment, one must have the same five good qualities. If one has these qualities, then regardless of gender, it is possible to attain Enlightenment. It need not take long to learn Buddha's teachings, for all humans possess a nature that has an affinity for Enlightenment.

2. In the practice of the way to Enlightenment, people see the Buddha with their own eyes and believe in Buddha with their own minds. The eyes that see Buddha and the mind that believes in Buddha are the same eyes and the same mind that, until that day, had wandered about in the world of birth and death.

If a king is plagued by bandits, he must find out where their camp is before he can attack them. So, when a man is beset by worldly passions, he should first ascertain their origin.

When a man is in a house and opens his eyes he will first notice the interior of the room and only later will he see the view outside the windows. In like manner we cannot have the eye notice external things before there is recognition by the eye of the things in the house.

If there is a mind within the body, it ought first to know the things inside the body; but generally people are interested in external things and seem to know or care little for the things within the body.

If the mind is located outside the body, it should not be in contact with the needs of the body. But, in fact, the body feels what the mind knows, and the mind knows what the body feels. Therefore, it cannot be said that the human mind is outside of the body. Where, then, does the substance of the mind exist?

3. From the unknown past, being conditioned by their own deeds and deluded by two fundamental misconceptions, people have wandered about in ignorance.

First, they believed that the discriminating mind, which lies at the root of this life of birth and death, was their real nature; and, second, they did not know that, hidden behind the discriminating mind, they possessed a pure mind of Enlightenment which is their true nature.

When a man closes his fist and raises his arm, the eyes see it and the mind discriminates it, but the mind that discriminates it is not the true mind.

The discriminating mind is only a mind for the discrimination of imagined differences that greed and other moods relating to the self have created. The discriminating mind is subject to causes and conditions, it is empty of any self-substance, and it is constantly changing. But, since people believe that this mind is their real mind, the delusion enters into the causes and conditions that produce suffering.

A man opens his hand and the mind perceives it; but what is it that moves? Is it the mind, or is it the hand? Or is it neither of them? If the hand moves, then the mind moves accordingly, and vice versa; but the moving mind is only a superficial appearance of mind: it is not the true and fundamental mind.

4.   Fundamentally, everyone has a pure clean mind, but it is usually covered by the defilement and dust of worldly desires which have arisen from one's circumstances. This defiled mind is not of the essence of one's nature: something has been added, like an intruder or even a guest in a home, but not its host.

The moon is often hidden by clouds, but it is not moved by them and its purity remains untarnished. Therefore, people must not be deluded into thinking that this defiled mind is their own true mind.

They must continually remind themselves of this fact by striving to awaken within themselves the pure and unchanging fundamental mind of Enlightenment. Being caught by a changing, defiled mind and being deluded by their own perverted ideas, they wander about in a world of delusion.

The disturbances and defilements of the human mind are aroused by greed as well as by its reactions to the changing circumstances.

The mind that is not disturbed by things as they occur, that remains pure and tranquil under all circumstances, is the true mind and should be the master.

We cannot say an inn disappears just because the guest is out of sight; neither can we say that the true self has disappeared when the defiled mind which has been aroused by the changing circumstances of life has disappeared. That which changes with changing conditions is not the true nature of mind.

5. Let us think of a lecture hall that is bright while the sun is shining but is dark after the sun goes down.

We can think of the light departing with the sun and the dark coming with the night, but we cannot so think of the mind that perceives lightness and darkness. The mind that is susceptible to lightness and darkness cannot be given back to anybody; it can only revert to a truer nature which is its fundamental nature.

It is only a "temporary" mind that momentarily notes changes of lightness and darkness as the sun rises and sets.

It is only a "temporary" mind that has different feelings from moment to moment with the changing circumstances of life; it is not the real and true mind. The fundamental and true mind which realises the lightness and the darkness is the true nature of man.

The temporary feelings of good and evil, love and hatred, that have been aroused by surroundings and changing external conditions, are only momentary reactions that have their cause in the defilement accumulated by the human mind.

Behind the desires and worldly passions which the mind entertains, there abides, clear and undefiled, the fundamental and true essence of mind.

Water is round in a round receptacle and square in a square one, but water itself has no particular shape. People often forget this fact.

People see this good and that bad, they like this and dislike that, and they discriminate existence from nonexistence; and then, being caught in these entanglements and becoming attached to them, they suffer.

If people would only give up their attachments to these imaginary and false discriminations, and restore the purity of their original minds, then both their mind and their body would be free from defilement and suffering; they would know the peacefulness that comes with that freedom.

II

Buddha-Nature

1. We have spoken of the pure and true mind as being fundamental; it is the Buddha-nature, that is, the seed of Buddhahood.

One can get fire if one holds a lens between the sun and moxa, but where does the fire come from? The lens is at an enormous distance from the sun, but the fire certainly appears upon the moxa by means of the lens. But if the moxa would not have the nature to kindle, there would be no fire.

In like manner, if the light of Buddha's Wisdom is concentrated upon the human mind, its true nature, which is Buddhahood, will be enkindled, and its light will illuminate the minds of the people with its brightness, and will awaken faith in Buddha. He holds the lens of Wisdom before all human minds and their faith may be quickened.

2. Often people disregard the affinity of their true minds for Buddha's enlightened wisdom, and, because of it, are caught by the entanglement of worldly passions, becoming attached to the discrimination of good and evil, and then lament over their bondage and suffering.

Why is it that people, possessing this fundamental and pure mind, should still cling to illusions and doom themselves to wander about in a world of delusion and suffering, covering their own Buddha-nature while all about them is the light of Buddha's Wisdom?

Once upon a time a man looked into the reverse side of a mirror and, seeing his face and head, he became insane. How unnecessary it is for a man to become insane merely because he carelessly looks into the reverse side of a mirror!

It is just as foolish and unnecessary for a person to go on suffering because he does not attain Enlightenment where he expects to find it. There is no failure in Enlightenment; the failure lies in those people who, for a long time, have sought Enlightenment in their discriminating minds, not realizing that theirs are not true minds but are imaginary minds that have been caused by the accumulation of greed and illusion covering and hiding their true mind.

If the accumulation of false beliefs is cleared away, Enlightenment will appear. But, strange enough, when people attain Enlightenment, they will realise that without false beliefs there could be no Enlightenment.

3.   Buddha-nature is not something that comes to an end. Though wicked men should be born beasts or angry demons, or fall into hell, they never lose their Buddha-nature.

However buried in the defilement of flesh or concealed at the root of worldly desires and forgotten it may be, the human affinity for Buddhahood is never completely extinguished.

4.   There is an old story of a man who fell into a drunken sleep. His friend stayed by him as long as he could but, being compelled to go and fearing that he might be in want, the friend hid a jewel in the drunken man's garment. When the drunken man recovered, not knowing that his friend had hid a jewel in his garment, he wandered about in poverty and hunger. A long time afterwards the two men met again and the friend told the poor man about the jewel and advised him to look for it.

Like the drunken man of the story, people wander about suffering in this life of birth and death, unconscious of what is hidden away in their inner nature, pure and untarnished, the priceless treasure of Buddha-nature.

However unconscious people may be of the fact that everyone has within his possession this supreme nature, and however degraded and ignorant they may be, Buddha never loses faith in them because He knows that even in the least of them there are, potentially, all the virtues of Buddhahood.

So Buddha awakens faith in them who are deceived by ignorance and cannot see their own Buddha-nature, leads them

away from their illusions and teaches them that originally there
is no difference between themselves and Buddhahood.

5.   Buddha is one who has attained Buddhahood and people
are those who are capable of attaining Buddhahood; that is all
the difference that lies between them.

But if a man thinks that he has attained Enlightenment, he
is deceiving himself, for, although he may be moving in that
direction, he has not yet reached Buddhahood.

Buddha-nature does not appear without diligent and
faithful effort, nor is the task finished until Buddhahood is
attained.

6.   Once upon a time a king gathered some blind men about
an elephant and asked them to tell him what an elephant was
like. The first man felt a tusk and said an elephant was like a
giant carrot; another happened to touch an ear and said it was
like a big fan; another touched its trunk and said it was like a
pestle; still another, who happened to feel its leg, said it was
like a mortar; and another, who grasped its tail said it was like
a rope. Not one of them was able to tell the king the elephant's
real form.

In like manner, one might partially describe the nature of
man but would not be able to describe the true nature of a
human being, the Buddha-nature.

There is only one possible way by which the everlasting
nature of man, his Buddha-nature, that cannot be disturbed by
worldly desires or destroyed by death, can be realised, and
that is by the Buddha and the Buddha's noble teachings.

III

Egolessness

1.   We have been speaking of Buddha-nature as though it
were something that could be described, as though it were
similar to the "soul" of other teachings, but it is not.

The concept of an "ego-personality" is something that has been imagined by a discriminating mind which first grasped it and then became attached to it, but which must abandon it. On the contrary, Buddha-nature is something indescribable that must first be discovered. In one sense, it resembles an "ego-personality" but it is not the "ego" in the sense of "I am" or "mine".

To believe in the existence of an ego is an erroneous belief that supposes the existence of nonexistence; to deny Buddha-nature is wrong, for it supposes that existence is nonexistence. This can be explained in a parable. A mother took her sick child to a doctor. The doctor gave the child medicine and instructed the mother not to nurse the child until the medicine was digested.

The mother anointed her breast with something bitter so that the child would keep away from her of his own volition. After the medicine had had enough time to be digested, the mother cleansed her breast and nursed the child. The mother took this method of saving her child out of kindness because she loved the child.

Like the mother in the parable, Buddha, in order to remove misunderstanding and to break up attachments to an ego-personality, denies the existence of an ego; and when the misunderstanding and attachments are done away with, then He explains the reality of the true mind that is the Buddha-nature.

Attachment to an ego-personality leads people into delusions, but faith in their Buddha-nature leads them to Enlightenment.

It is like the woman in a story to whom a chest was bequeathed. Not knowing that the chest contained gold, she continued to live in poverty until another person opened it and showed her the gold. Buddha opens the minds of people and shows them the purity of their Buddha-nature.

2. If everyone has this Buddha-nature, why is there so much suffering from people cheating one another or killing one

another? And why are there so many distinctions of rank and wealth, rich and poor?

There is a story of a wrestler who used to wear an ornament on his forehead comprising a precious stone. Once when he was wrestling the stone was crushed into the flesh of his forehead. He thought he had lost the gem and went to a surgeon to have the wound dressed. When the surgeon came to dress the wound he found the gem embedded in the flesh and covered with blood and dirt. He held up a mirror and showed the stone to the wrestler.

Buddha-nature is like the precious stone of this story: it becomes covered over by the dirt and dust of other interests and people think that they have lost it, but a good teacher recovers it again for them.

Like the wrestler in the story who was shown the gem buried in his flesh and blood by means of a mirror, so people are shown their Buddha-nature, buried beneath their worldly desires and passions, by means of the light of Buddha.

3. Buddha-nature is always pure and tranquil no matter how varied the conditions and surroundings of people may be. Just as milk is always white regardless of the colour of the cow's hide; either red, white, or black, so it does not matter how differently their deeds may condition people's life or what different effects may follow their acts and thoughts.

There is a fable told in India of a mysterious medical herb that was hidden under the tall grasses of the Himalayas. For a long time men sought for it in vain, but at last a wise man located it by its sweetness. As long as the wise man lived they collected this medical herb in a tub, but after his death, the sweet elixir remained hidden in some far-off spring in the mountains, and the water in the tub turned sour and harmful and of a different taste.

In like manner Buddha-nature is hidden away beneath the wild growth of worldly passions and can rarely be discovered, but Buddha found it and revealed it to the people, and as they receive it by their varying faculties it tastes differently to each person.

4. The diamond, the hardest of known substances, cannot be crushed. Sand and stones can be ground to powder but diamonds remain unscathed. Buddha-nature is like the diamond, and thus cannot be broken.

Human nature, both its body and mind, will wear away, but the nature of Buddhahood cannot be destroyed.

Buddha-nature is, indeed, the most excellent characteristic of human nature. Buddha teaches that, although in human nature there may be endless varieties such as men and women, there is no discrimination with regard to Buddha-nature.

Pure gold is procured by melting ore and removing all impure substances. If people would melt the ore of their minds and remove all the impurities of worldly passion and egoism, they would all recover the same pure Buddha-nature.

Chapter Four

Defilements

I

Human Defilements

1. There are two kinds of worldly passions that defile and cover the purity of Buddha-nature.

The first is the passion for analysis and discussion by which people become confused in judgement. The second is the passion for emotional experience by which people's values become confused.

Both delusions of reasoning and of practice can be thought of as a classification of all human defilements, but really there are two original worldly predicaments in their bases. The first is ignorance, and the second is desire.

The delusions of reasoning are based upon ignorance, and the delusions of practice are based upon desire, so that the two sets are really one set after all, and together they are the source of all unhappiness.

If people are ignorant they cannot reason correctly and safely. As they yield to a desire for existence, graspings, clingings and attachments to everything inevitably follow. It is this constant hunger for every pleasant thing seen and heard that leads people into the delusions of habit. Some people even yield to the desire for the death of the body.

From these primary sources all greed, anger, foolishness, misunderstanding, resentment, jealousy, flattery, deceit, pride, contempt, inebriety, selfishness, have their generations and appearances.

2. Greed rises from wrong ideas of satisfaction; anger rises from wrong ideas concerning the state of one's affairs and surroundings; foolishness rises from the inability to judge what correct conduct is.

These three – greed, anger and foolishness – are called the three fires of the world. The fire of greed consumes those who have lost their true minds through greed; the fire of anger consumes those who have lost their true minds through anger; the fire of foolishness consumes those who have lost their true minds through their failure to hear and to heed the teachings of Buddha.

Indeed, this world is burning up with its many and various fires. There are fires of greed, fires of anger, fires of foolishness, fires of infatuation and egoism, fires of decrepitude, sickness and death, fires of sorrow, lamentation, suffering and agony. Everywhere these fires are raging. They not only burn the self, but also cause others to suffer and lead them into wrong acts of body, speech and mind. From the wounds that are caused by these fires there issues a pus that infects and poisons those who approach it, and leads them into evil paths.

3. Greed rises in want of satisfaction; anger rises in want of dissatisfaction; and foolishness rises from impure thoughts. The evil of greed has little impurity but is hard to remove; the evil of foolishness has much impurity and is very hard to overcome.

Therefore, people should quench these fires whenever and wherever they appear by correctly judging as to what can give true satisfaction, by correctly controlling the mind in the face of the unsatisfactory things of life, and by ever recalling Buddha's teachings of goodwill and kindness. If the mind is filled with wise and pure and unselfish thoughts, there will be no place for worldly passions to take root.

4. Greed, anger and foolishness are like a fever. If a man gets this fever, even if he lies in a comfortable room, he will suffer and be tormented by sleeplessness.

Those who have no such fever have no difficulty in sleeping peacefully, even on a cold winter night, on the ground with only a thin covering of leaves, or on a hot summer's night in a small closed room.

These three – greed, anger and foolishness – are, therefore, the sources of all human woe. To get rid of these sources of woe, one must observe the precepts, must practise concentration of mind and must have wisdom. Observance of the precepts will remove the impurities of greed; right concentration of mind will remove the impurities of anger; and wisdom will remove the impurities of foolishness.

5. Human desires are endless. It is like the thirst of a man who drinks salt water: he gets no satisfaction and his thirst is only increased.

So it is with a man who seeks to gratify his desires; he only gains increased dissatisfaction and his woes are multiplied.

The gratification of desires never satisfies; it always leaves behind unrest and irritation that can never be allayed, and then, if the gratification of his desires is thwarted, it will often drive him "insane".

To satisfy their desires, people will struggle and fight with each other, king against king, vassal against vassal, parent against child, brother against brother, sister against sister, friend against friend; they will fight and even kill each other to satisfy their desires.

They will sin with their own bodies and words, sin with their own minds, knowing perfectly well that the gratification will ultimately bring unhappiness and suffering, so imperious is desire. And then, the various sufferings in the following world and the agonies of falling into it follow.

6. Of all the worldly passions, lust is the most intense. All other worldly passions seem to follow in its train.

Lust seems to provide the soil in which other passions flourish. Lust is like a demon that eats up all the good deeds of the world. Lust is a viper hiding in a flower garden; it poisons those who come in search only of beauty. Lust is a vine that climbs a tree and spreads over the branches until the tree is strangled. Lust insinuates its tentacles into human emotions and sucks away the good sense of the mind until the mind withers. Lust is a bait cast by the evil demon that foolish people snap at and are dragged down by into the depths of the evil world.

If a dry bone is smeared with blood a dog will gnaw at it until he is tired and frustrated. Lust to a man is precisely like this bone to a dog; he will covet it until he is exhausted.

If a single piece of meat is thrown to two wild beasts they will fight and claw each other to get it. A man foolish enough to carry a torch against the wind is likely to burn himself. Like these two beasts and this foolish man, people hurt and burn themselves because of their worldly desires.

7.   It is easy to shield the outer body from poisoned arrows, but it is impossible to shield the mind from the poisoned darts that originate within itself. Greed, anger, foolishness and the infatuations of egoism – these four poisoned darts originate within the mind and infect it with deadly poison.

If people are infected with greed, anger and foolishness, they will lie, cheat, abuse and be double-tongued, and, then will actualize their words by killing, stealing and committing adultery.

These three evil states of mind, the four evil utterances, and the three evil acts, if added together, become the ten gross evils.

If people become accustomed to lying, they will unconsciously commit every possible wrong deed. Before they can act wickedly they must lie, and once they begin to lie they will act wickedly with unconcern.

Greed, lust, fear, anger, misfortune and unhappiness all derive from foolishness. Thus, foolishness is the greatest of the poisons.

8. From desire action follows; from action suffering follows; desire, action and suffering are like a wheel rotating endlessly and forming the vicious circle.

The rolling of this wheel has no beginning and no end; people cannot escape such reincarnation. One life follows another life according to this transmigrating cycle in endless recurrence.

If one were to pile the ashes and bones of himself burnt in this everlasting, the pile would be mountain high; if one were to collect the milk of mothers which he suckled during his transmigration, it would be deeper than the sea.

Although the nature of Buddhahood is possessed by all people, it is buried so deeply in the defilements of worldly passion that it long remains unknown. That is why suffering is so universal and why there is this endless recurrence of miserable lives.

But, just as by yielding to greed, anger and foolishness, evil deeds are accumulated and condition rebirth, so, by following the Buddha's teachings, the evil sources will be cleared away rebirth in the world of suffering will be ended.

II
Man's Nature

1. Man's nature is like a dense thicket that has no entrance and is difficult to penetrate. In comparison, the nature of an animal is much easier to understand. Still, we can in a general way classify the nature of man according to four outstanding differences.

First, there are those who, because of wrong teachings, practise austerities and cause themselves to suffer. Second, there are those who, by cruelty, by stealing, by killing, or by other unkind acts, cause others to suffer. Along with themselves. Fourth, there are those who do not suffer themselves and save others from suffering. These people of the last category, by following the teachings of Buddha, do not give way to greed, anger or foolishness, but live peaceful lives of kindness and wisdom without killing or stealing.

2.   There are three kinds of people in the world. The first are those who are like letters carved in rock; they easily give way to anger and retain their angry thoughts for a long time. The second are those who are like letters written in sand; they give way to anger also, but their angry thoughts quickly pass away. The third is those who are like letters written in running water; they do not retain their passing thoughts; they let abuse and uncomfortable gossip pass by unnoticed; their minds are always pure and undisturbed.

There are three other kinds of people. The first are those who are proud, act rashly and are never satisfied; their natures are easy to understand. Then there are those who are courteous and always act after consideration; their natures are hard to understand. Then there are those who have overcome desire completely; it is impossible to understand their natures.

Thus people can be classified in many different ways, but nevertheless, their natures are hard to understand. Only Buddha understands them, and by His wisdom, leads them through varied teachings.

III

Human Life

1.   There is an allegory that depicts human life. Once there was a man rowing a boat down a river. Someone on the shore warned him, "Stop rowing so gaily down the swift current; there are rapids ahead and a dangerous whirlpool, and there are crocodiles and demons lying in wait in rocky caverns. You will perish if you continue."

In this allegory, "the swift current" is a life of lust; "rowing gaily" is giving rein to one's passion; "rapids ahead" means the ensuing suffering and pain; "whirlpool" means pleasure, "crocodiles and demons" refers to the decay and death that follow a life of lust and indulgence; "Someone on the shore," who calls out, is Buddha.

Here is another allegory. A man who has committed a crime is running away; some guards are following him, so he tries to hide himself by descending into a well by means of some vines growing down the sides. As he descends he sees vipers at the bottom of the wells, so he decides to cling to the vine for safety. After a time when his arms are getting tired, he notices two mice, one white and the other black, gnawing at the vine.

If the vine breaks, he will fall to the vipers and perish. Suddenly, on looking upward, he notices just above his face a beehive from which occasionally falls a drop of honey. The man, forgetting all his danger, tastes the honey with delight.

A "man" means the one who is born to suffer and to die alone. "Guards" and "vipers" refer to the body with all its desires. "Vines" means the continuity of the human life. "Two mice, one white and the other black" refer to the duration of time, days and nights, and the passing years. "Honey" indicates the physical pleasures that beguiles the suffering of the passing years.

2.   Here is still another allegory. A king places four vipers in a box and gives the box into the safekeeping of a servant. He commands the servant to take good care of them and warns that if he angers even one of them he will be punished with death. The servant, in fear, decides to throw away the box and escape.

The king sends five guards to capture the servant. At first they approach the servant in a friendly manner, intending to take him back safely, but the servant does not trust their friendliness and escapes to another village.

Then, in a vision, a voice tells him that in this village there is no safe shelter, and that there are six bandits who will attack him, so the servant runs away in fright until he comes to a wild river that blocks his way. Thinking of the dangers that are following him, he makes a raft and succeeds in crossing the turbulent current, beyond which he finally finds safety and peace.

"Four vipers in a box" indicate the four elements of earth, water, fire and air that make up the body of flesh. The body is given into the charge of lust and is an enemy of the mind. Therefore, he tries to run away from the body.

"Five guards who approach in friendly manner" mean the five aggregates – form, feeling, perception, volition and consciousness – which frame body and mind.

"The safe shelter" is the six senses, which are no safe shelter after all, and "the six bandits" are the six objects of the six senses. Thus, seeing the dangers within the six senses, he runs away once more and comes to the wild current of worldly desires.

Then he makes himself a raft of the Buddha's good teachings and crosses the wild current safely.

3. There are three occasions full of perils when a son is helpless to aid his mother and a mother cannot help her son – a fire, a flood and a burglary. Yet, even on these perilous and sad occasions, there still exists a chance for aiding each other.

But there are three occasions when it is impossible for a mother to save her son or a son to save his mother. These three occasions are the time of sickness, the period of growing old, and the moment of death.

How can a son take his mother's place when she is growing old? How can a mother take her son's place when he is sick? How can either help the other when the moment of death approaches? No matter how much they love each other or how intimate they may have been, neither can help the other on such occasions.

4. Once Yama, the legendary king of Hell, asked a man who had fallen into hell about his evil deeds in life, whether, during his life, he had ever met the three heavenly messengers. The man replied: "No, my Lord. I never met any such persons.

Yama asked him if he had ever met an old person bent with age and walking with a cane. The man replied: "Yes, my Lord, I have met such persons frequently." Then Yama said to

him: "You are suffering this present punishment because you
did not recognise in that old man a heavenly messenger sent to
warn you that you must quickly change your ways before you,
too, become and old man."

Yama asked him again if he had ever seen a poor, sick and
friendless man. The man replied: "Yes, my Lord, I have seen
many such men." Then, Yama said to him: "You have come
into this place because you failed to recognise in these sick
men the messengers from heaven sent to warn you of your
own sickness."

Then, Yama asked him once more if he had ever seen dead
man. The man replied: "Yes, my Lord, I have been in the
presence of death many times." Yama said to him: "It is
because you did not recognise in these men the heavenly
messengers sent to warn you that you are brought to this. If
you had recognised these messengers and taken their warnings
you would have changed your course, and would not have
come to this place of suffering."

5.   Once there was a young woman named Kisagotami, the
wife of a wealthy man, who lost her mind because of the death
of her child. She took the dead child in her arms and went
from house to house begging people to heal the child.

Of course, they could do nothing for her, but finally a
follower of Buddha advised her to see the Blessed One who
was then staying at Jetavana, and so she carried the dead child
to Buddha.

The Blessed One looked upon her with sympathy and said:
"To heal the child I need some poppy seeds; go and beg four
or five poppy seeds from some home where death has never
entered."

So the demented woman went out and sought a house
where death had never entered, but in vain. At last, she was
obliged to return to Buddha. In his quiet presence her mind
cleared and she understood the meaning of his words. She
took the body away and buried it, and then returned to Buddha
and became one of his disciples.

IV

Reality of Human Life

1. People in this world are prone to be selfish and unsympathetic; they do not know how to love and respect one another; they argue and quarrel over trifling affairs only to their own harm and suffering, and life becomes but a dreary round of unhappiness.

Regardless of whether they are rich or poor, they worry about money; they suffer from poverty and they suffer from wealth. Because their lives are controlled by greed, they are never contented, never satisfied.

A wealthy man worries about his estate if he has one; he worries lest some disaster befall him, his mansion burns down, robbers break in, kidnappers carry him off. Then he worries about death and the disposition of his wealth. Indeed, his way to death is lonely, and nobody follows him to death.

A poor man always suffers from insufficiency and this serves to awaken endless desires – for land and a house. Being aflamed with covetousness he wears out both his body and mind, and comes to death in the middle of his life.

The whole world seems pitted against him and even the path to death seems lonesome as though he has a long journey to make and no friends to keep him company.

2. Now, there are five evils in the world. First, there is cruelty; every creature, even insects, strives against one another. The strong attack the weak; the weak deceive the strong; everywhere there is fighting and cruelty.

Second, there is the lack of a clear demarcation between the rights of a father and a son; between an elder brother and a younger; between a husband and a wife; between a senior relative and a younger; on every occasion each one desires to be the highest and to profit at the cost of others. They cheat each other, there is deception and a lack of sincerity.

Third, there is the lack of a clear demarcation as to the behaviour between men and women. Everyone at times has impure and lascivious thoughts and desires that lead them into questionable acts and often into disputes, fighting, injustice and wickedness.

Fourth, there is the tendency for people to disrespect the rights of others, to exaggerate their own importance at the expense of others, to set bad examples of behaviour and, being unjust in their speech, to deceive, slander and abuse others.

Fifth, there is the tendency for people to neglect their duties toward others. They think too much of their own comfort and their own desires; they forget the favours they have received and cause annoyance to others that often passes into great injustice.

3. People should have more sympathy for one another, they should respect one another for their good traits and help one another in their difficulties; but, instead, they are selfish and hardhearted; they despise one anther for their failings and dislike others for their advantages. These aversions generally grow worse with time, and after a while, become intolerable.

Truly, in this world of lust, a man is born alone and dies alone, and there is no one to share his punishment in the life after death.

The law of cause and effect is universal; each man must carry his own burden of sin and must go along to its retribution. The same law of cause and effect controls good deeds. A life of sympathy and kindness will result in good fortune and happiness.

4. As years go by and people see how strongly they are bound by greed, habit and suffering, they become very sad and discouraged. Often in their discouragement they quarrel with others and sink deeper into sin and give up trying to walk the true path; often their lives come to some untimely end in the very midst of their wickedness and they suffer forever.

This falling into discouragement because of one's misfortunes and sufferings is most unnatural and contrary to the law of heaven and earth, and therefore, one will suffer both in this world and in the worlds after death.

It is true that everything in this life is transitory and filled with uncertainty, but it is lamentable that anyone should ignore this fact and keep on trying to seek enjoyment and satisfaction of his desires.

5. It is natural in this world of suffering for people to think and act selfishly and egoistically and, because of it, it is equally natural for suffering and unhappiness to follow.

People favour themselves and neglect others. People let their own desires run into greed and lust and all manner of evil. Because of these they must suffer endlessly.

6. Therefore, people should cast away, while they are young and healthy, all their greed and attachment to worldly affairs, and should seek earnestly for true Enlightenment, for there can be no lasting reliance or happiness apart from Enlightenment.

Most people, however, disbelieve or ignore this law of cause and effect. They go on in their habits of greed and selfishness, being oblivious of the fact that a good deed brings happiness and an evil deed brings misfortune. Nor do they really believe that one's acts in this with regard to the rewards and punishments for their sins.

They lament and cry about their sufferings, entirely misunderstanding the significance their present acts have upon their following lives and the relation their sufferings have to the acts of their previous lives. They think only of present desire and present suffering.

Nothing in the world is permanent or lasting; everything is changing and momentary and unpredictable. But people are ignorant and selfish, and are concerned only with the desires and sufferings of the passing moment. They do not listen to the good teachings nor do they try to understand them; they simply give themselves up to the present interest, to wealth and lust.

7. From time immemorial, an incalculable number of people have been born into this world of delusion and suffering, and they are still being born. It is fortunate, however, that the world has the Buddha's teachings and that men can believe in them and be helped.

Therefore, people should think deeply, should keep their minds pure and their bodies well, should keep away from greed and evil, and should seek good.

To us, fortunately, the knowledge of the Buddha's teachings has come; we should seek to believe in them and wish to be born in the Buddha's Pure Land. Knowing Buddha's teachings, we should not follow others into greedy and sinful ways, nor should we keep the Buddha's teachings to ourselves alone, but should practise the teachings and pass them on to others.

Chapter Five

The Relief Offered by Buddha

I

Amida Buddha's Vows

1. As already explained, people always yield to their worldly passions, repeating sin after sin, and carry burdens of intolerable acts, unaware of their own wisdom or of their own strength to break these habits of greed and indulgence. If they are unable to overcome and remove worldly passions, how can they expect to realise their true nature of Buddhahood?

Buddha, who thoroughly understood human nature, had great sympathy for men made a vow that He would do everything possible, even at the cost of great hardship to Himself, to relieve them of their fears and sufferings. To effect this relief He manifested himself as a Bodhisattva in the immemorable past and made the following ten vows:

(a) "Though I attain Buddhahood, I shall never be complete until everyone in my land is certain of entering Buddhahood and gaining Enlightenment.

(b) "Though I attain Buddhahood, I shall never be complete until my affirming light reaches all over the world.

(c) "Though I attain Buddhahood, I shall never be complete until my life endures through the ages and saves innumerable numbers of people.

(d) "Though I attain Buddhahood, I shall never be complete until all the Buddhas in the ten directions unite in praising my name.

(e) "Though I attain Buddhahood, I shall never be complete
until people with sincere faith endeavour to be reborn in
my land by repeating my name in sincere faith ten times
and actually do succeed in this rebirth.

(f) "Though I attain Buddhahood, I shall never be complete
until people everywhere determine to attain
Enlightenment, practise virtues, sincerely wish to be born
in my land; thus, I shall appear at the moment of their
death with a great company of Bodhisattvas to welcome
them into my Pure Land.

(g) "Though I attain Buddhahood, I shall never be complete
until people everywhere, hearing my name, think of my
land and wish to be born there and, to that end, sincerely
plant seeds of virtue, and are thus able to accomplish all to
their hearts' desire.

(h) "Though I attain Buddhahood, I shall never be complete
until all those who are born in my Pure Land are certain to
attain Buddhahood, so that they may lead many others to
Enlightenment and to the practice of great compassion.

(i) "Though I attain Buddhahood, I shall never be complete
until people all over the world are influenced by my spirit
of loving compassion that will purify their minds and
bodies and lift them above the things of the world.

(j) "Though I attain Buddhahood, I shall never be complete
until people everywhere, hearing my name, learn right
ideas about life and death, and gain that perfect wisdom
that will keep their minds pure and tranquil in the midst of
the world's greed and suffering.

"Thus I make these vows; may I not attain Buddhahood
until they are fulfilled. May I become the source of unlimited
Light, freeing and radiating the treasures of my wisdom and
virtue, enlightening all lands and emancipating all suffering
people."

2. Thus he, by accumulating innumerable virtues through
many eons of time, became Amida or the Buddha of Infinite
Light and Boundless Life, and perfected his own Buddha-land

of Purity, wherein He is now living, in a world of peace, enlightening all people.

This Pure Land, wherein there is no suffering, is, indeed, most peaceful and happy. Clothing, food and all beautiful things appear when those who live there wish for them. When a gentle breeze passes through its jewel-laden trees, the music of its holy teachings fills the air and cleanses the minds of all who listen to it.

In this Pure Land there are many fragrant lotus blossoms, and each blossom has many precious petals, and each petal shines with ineffable beauty. The radiance of these lotus blossoms brightens the path of Wisdom, and those who listen to the music of the holy teachings are led into perfect peace.

3. Now all the Buddhas of the ten directions are praising the virtues of this Buddha of Infinite Light and Boundless Life.

Whoever hears this Buddha's Name magnifies and receives it with joy, his mind becomes one with Buddha's mind and he will be born in the Buddha's wondrous Land of Purity.

Those who are born in that Pure Land share in Buddha's boundless life; their hearts are immediately filled with sympathy for all sufferers and they go forward to manifest the Buddha's method of salvation.

In the spirit of these vows they cast away all worldly attachments and realise the impermanence of this world. And they devote their merits to the emancipation of all sentient life; they integrate their own lives with the lives of all others, sharing their illusions and sufferings but, at the same time, realising their freedom the bonds and attachments of this worldly life.

They know the hindrances and difficulties of worldly living but they know, also, the boundless potentialities of Buddha's compassion. They are free to go or come, they are free to advance or to stop as they wish, but they choose to remain with those upon whom Buddha has compassion.

Therefore, if anyone hearing the name of this Amida Buddha is encouraged to call upon that name in perfect faith, he shall share in Buddha's compassion. So all people should listen to the Buddha's teachings and should follow it even if it seems to lead them again through the flames that envelop this world of life and death.

If people truly and earnestly wish to attain Enlightenment, they must rely on the power of this Buddha. It is impossible for an ordinary person to realise his supreme Buddha-nature without the support of this Buddha.

4. Amida Buddha is not far from anyone. His Land of Purity is described as being far away to the west but it is, also, within the minds of those who earnestly wish to be with him.

When some people picture in their minds the figure of Amida Buddha shining in golden splendour, the picture divides into eighty-four thousand figures or features, each figure or feature emitting eighty-four thousand rays of light and each ray of light, enlightening a world, never leaving in darkness a single person who is reciting the name of Buddha. Thus this Buddha helps people take advantage of the salvation He offers.

By seeing the image of Buddha, one is enabled to realise the mind of Buddha. The Buddha's mind has great compassion that includes all, even those who are ignorant of his compassion or forgetful of it, and particularly those who remember it in faith.

To those who have faith, He offers the opportunity to become one with Him. As this Buddha is the all-inclusive body of equality, whoever thinks of Buddha, Buddha thinks of him and enters his mind freely.

This means that, when a person thinks of Buddha, he has Buddha's mind in all its pure, happy and peaceful perfection. In other words, his mind is a Buddha-mind.

Therefore, each man in purity and sincerity of faith, should picture his own mind as being Buddha's mind.

5. Buddha has many forms of transfiguration and incarnation, and can manifest Himself in manifold ways according to the ability of each person.

He manifests his body in immense size to cover all the sky and stretches away into the boundless stellar spaces. He also manifests Himself in the infinitesimal of nature, sometimes in forms, sometimes in energy, sometimes in aspects of mind, and sometimes in personality.

But in some manner or other, He will surely appear to those who recite the name of Buddha with faith. To such, Amida always appears accompanied by two Bodhisattvas: Avalokitesvara, the Bodhisattva of compassion and Mahasthama-prapta, the Bodhisattva of Wisdom. His manifestations fill up the world for everyone to see but only those who have faith notice them.

Those who are able to see His temporal manifestations acquire abiding satisfaction and happiness. Moreover, those who are able to see the real Buddha realise incalculable fortunes of joy and peace.

6. Since the mind of Amida Buddha with all its boundless potentialities of love and wisdom is compassion itself, Buddha can save all.

The most wicked of people – those who commit unbelievable crimes, whose minds are filled with greed, anger and infatuation; those who lie, chatter, abuse and cheat; those who kill, steal act lasciviously; those who are near the end of their lives after years of evil deeds – they are destined to long ages of punishment.

A good friend comes to them and pleads with them at their last moment, saying, "You are now facing death; you cannot blot out your life of wickedness, but you can take refuge in the compassion of the Buddha of Infinite Light by reciting His Name.

If these wicked men recite the holy name of Amida Buddha with singleness of mind, all the sins which would have destined them to the evil world will be cleared away.

If simply repeating that holy name can do this, how much more would be possible if one is able to concentrate his mind upon this Buddha!

Those who are thus able to recite the holy name, when they come to the end of life, will be met by Amida Buddha and the Bodhisattvas of Compassion and Wisdom and will be led by them into the Buddha's Land, where they will be born in all purity of the white lotus.

Therefore, everyone should keep in mind the words, "Namu-Amida-Butsu" or Whole-hearted Reliance upon the Buddha of Infinite Light and Boundless Life!

II

Amida Buddha's Land of Purity

1. The Buddha of Infinite Light and Boundless Life is ever living and ever radiating His Truth. In His Pure Land there is no suffering and no darkness, and every hour is passed in joy; therefore, it is called the Land of Bliss.

In the midst of this Land there is a lake of pure water, fresh and sparkling, whose waves lap softly on shores of golden sands. Here and there are huge lotus blossoms as large as chariot wheels of many and various lights and colours – blue lights from blue colour, yellow for yellow, red for red, white for white – whose fragrance fills the air.

At different places on the margin of the lake there are pavilions decorated with gold and silver, lapis lazuli and crystal, with marble steps leading down to the water's edge. At other places there are parapets and balustrades hanging over the water and enclosed with curtains and networks of precious gems, and in between there are groves of spices trees and flowering shrubs.

The ground is shining with beauty and the air is vibrant with celestial harmonies. Six times during the day and night, delicately tinted flower petals fall from the sky and people gather them and carry them in flower vessels to all the other Buddha-lands and make offerings of them to the myriad Buddhas.

2. In this wondrous Land there are many birds. There are snow-white storks and swans, and gaily coloured peacocks and tropical birds of paradise, and flocks of little birds, softly singing. In the Buddha's Pure Land these sweetly singing birds are voicing Buddha's teachings and praising His virtues.

Whoever hears and listens to the music of these voices, listens to the Buddha's voice and awakens to a newness of faith, joy and peace in fellowship with the brotherhood of followers everywhere.

Soft zephyrs pass through the tress of that Pure Land and stir the fragrant curtains of the Pavilions and pass away in sweet cadences of music.

People hearing faint echoes of this heavenly music think of the Buddha, of the Dharma (teaching), and of the Samgha (brotherhood). All these excellences are but reflections of the Pure Land.

3. Why is Buddha in this land called Amida, indicating the Buddha of Infinite Light and Boundless Life? It is because the splendour of His Truth radiates unimpeded to the outermost and innermost limits of the Buddha-lands; it is because the vitality of His living compassion never wanes through the incalculable lives and eons of time.

It is because the number of those who are born in His Pure Land and are perfectly enlightened is incalculable and they will never again return to the world of delusions and death.

It is because the number of those who are awakened into the newness of Life by His lights is also incalculable.

Therefore, should all people concentrate their minds on His Name and, as they come toward the end of life, even for one day or seven days, recite Amida Buddha's Name in perfect faith, and they do this with undisturbed mind, they will be born in the Buddha's Land of Purity, being led by Amida Buddha and many other holy ones who appear at this last moment.

If any man hears Amida Buddha's Name, awakens his faith in His teachings, he will be able to attain unsurpassed perfect Enlightenment.

Part – III
THE WAY OF PRACTICE

Chapter One

The Way of Purification

I

Purification of the Mind

1. People have worldly passions which lead them into delusions and sufferings. There are five ways to emancipate themselves from the bond of worldly passions.

First, they should have right ideas of things, ideas that are based on careful observation, and understand causes and effects and their significance correctly. Since the cause of suffering desire and attachment are related to mistaken observations by an ego-self, neglecting the significance of the law of cause and effect, and since it is from these wrong observations, there can be peace only if the mind can be rid of these worldly passions.

Second, people can get rid of these mistaken observations and resulting worldly passions by careful and patient mind-control. With efficient mind-control they can avoid desires arising from the stimulation of the eyes, ears, nose, tongue, skin and the subsequent mental processes and, by so doing, cut off the very root of all worldly passions.

Third, they should have correct ideas with regard to the proper use of all things. That is, with regard to articles of food and clothing, they should not think of them in relation to comfort and pleasure, but only in their relation to the body's need. Clothing is necessary to protect the body against extremes of heat and cold, and to conceal the shame of the body; while it is training for Enlightenment and Buddhahood. Worldly passions cannot arise through such thinking.

Fourth, people should learn endurance; they should learn to endure the discomforts of heat and cold, hunger and thirst; they should learn to be patient when receiving abuse and scorn; for it is the practice of endurance that quenches the fire of worldly passions which is burning up their bodies.

Fifth, people should learn to see and so avoid all danger. Just as a wise man keeps away from wild horses or mad dogs, so one should not make friends with evil men, nor should he go to places that wise men avoid. If one practises caution and prudence, the fire of worldly passions which is burning in their vitals will die down.

2.   There are five groups of desires in the world.

Desires arising from the forms the eyes see; from the sounds the ears hear; from the fragrances the nose smells; from tastes pleasant to the tongue; from things that are agreeable to the sense of touch. From these five doors to desire come the body's love of comfort.

Most people, being influenced by the body's love of comfort, do not notice the evils that follow comfort, and they are caught in a devil's trap like a deer in the forest caught in a hunter's trap. Indeed, these five doors of desires arising from the senses are the most dangerous traps. When caught by them, people are entangled in worldly passions and suffer. They should know how to get rid of these traps.

3.   There is no one way to get free from the trap of worldly passions. Suppose you caught a snake, a crocodile, a bird, a dog, a fox and a monkey, six creatures of very different natures, and you tie them together with a strong rope and let them go. Each of these six creatures will try to go back to its own lair by its own method: the snake will seek a covering of grass, the crocodile will seek water, the bird will want to fly in the air, the dog will seek a village, the fox will seek the solitary ledges, and the monkey will seek the trees of a forest. In the attempt of each to go its own way there will be a struggle, but,

being tied together by a rope, the strongest at any one time will drag the rest.

Like the creatures in this parable, man is tempted in different ways by the desires of his six senses, eyes, ears, nose, tongue, touch and mind, and is controlled by the predominant desire.

If the six creatures are all tied to a post, they will try to get free until they are tired out, and then will lie down by the post. Just like this, if people will train and control the mind there will be no further trouble from the other five senses. If the mind is under control people will have happiness both now and in the future.

4. People love their egoistic comfort, which is a love of fame and praise. But fame and praise are like incense that consumes itself and soon disappears. If people chase after honours and public acclaim and leave the way of truth, they are in serious danger and will soon have cause for regret.

A man who chases after fame and wealth and love affairs is like a child who licks honey from the blade of a knife. While he is tasting the sweetness of honey, he has to risk hurting his tongue. He is like a man who carries a torch against a strong wind; the flame will surely burn his hands and face.

One must not trust his own mind that is filled with greed, anger and foolishness. One must not let his mind run free, but must keep it under strict control.

5. To attain perfect mind-control is a most difficult thing. Those who seek Enlightenment must first rid themselves of the fire of all desires. Desire is a raging fire, and one seeking Enlightenment must avoid the fire of desire as a man carrying a load of hay avoids sparks.

But it would be foolish for a man to put out his eyes for fear of being tempted by beautiful forms. The mind is master and if the mind is under control, the weaker desires will disappear.

It is difficult to follow the way to Enlightenment, but it is more difficult if people have no mind to seek such a way. Without Enlightenment, there is endless suffering in this world of life and death.

When a man seeks the way to Enlightenment, it is like an ox carrying a heavy load through a field of mud. If the ox tries to do its best without paying attention to other things, it can overcome the mud and take a rest. Just so, if the mind is controlled and kept on the right path, there will be no mud of greed to hinder it and all its suffering will disappear.

6. Those who seek the path to Enlightenment must first remove all egoistic pride and be humbly willing to accept the light of Buddha's teachings. All the treasures of the world, all its gold and silver and honours, are not to be compared with wisdom and virtue.

To enjoy good health, to bring true happiness to one's family, to bring peace to all, one must first discipline and control one's own mind. If a man can control his mind he can find the way to Enlightenment, and all wisdom and virtue will naturally come to him.

Just as treasures are uncovered from the earth, so virtue appears from good deeds, and wisdom appears from a pure and peaceful mind. To walk safely through the maze of human life, one needs the light of wisdom and the guidance of virtue.

The Buddha's teachings, which tells people how to eliminate greed, anger and foolishness, is a good teaching and those who follow it attain the happiness of a good life.

7. Human beings tend to move in the direction of their thoughts. If they harbour greedy thoughts, they become more greedy; if they think angry thoughts, they become more angry; if they hold foolish thoughts, their feet move in that direction.

At harvest time farmers keep their herds confined, lest they break through the fences into the field and give cause for complaint or for being killed; so people must closely guard their minds against dishonesty and misfortune. They must eliminate thoughts that stimulate greed, anger and foolishness, but encourage thoughts that stimulate charity and kindness.

When spring comes and the pastures have an abundance of green grass, farmers turn their cattle loose; but even then they keep a close watch over them. It is so with the minds of people: even under the best of conditions the mind will bear watching.

8. At one time Shakyamuni Buddha was staying in the town of Kausambi. In this town there was one who resented Him and who bribed wicked men to circulate false stories about Him. Under these circumstances it was difficult for His disciples to get sufficient food from their begging and there was much abuse in that town.

Ananda said to Shakyamuni: "We had better not stay in a town like this. There are other and better towns to go to. We had better leave this town."

The Blessed One replied: "Suppose the next town is like this, what shall we do then?"

"Then we move to another."

The Blessed One said: "No, Ananda, there will be no end in that way. We had better remain here and hear the abuse patiently until it ceases, and we move to another place.

"There are profit and loss, slander and honour, praise and abuse, suffering and pleasure in this world; the Enlightened One is not controlled by these external things; they will cease as quickly as they come."

II

The Good Way of Behaviour

1. Those who seek the way of Enlightenment must always bear in mind the necessity of constantly keeping their body, speech and mind pure. To keep the body pure one must not kill any living creature, one must not steal or commit adultery. To keep speech pure one must not lie, or abuse, or deceive, or

indulge in idle talk. To keep the mind pure one must remove all greed, anger and false judgement.

If the mind becomes impure, for sure, one's deeds will be impure; if the deeds are impure, there will be suffering. So it is of the greatest importance that the mind and the body be kept pure.

2. Once there was a rich widow who had a reputation for kindness, modesty and courtesy. She had a housemaid who was wise and diligent.

One day the maid thought: 'My mistress has a very good reputation; I wonder whether she is good by nature, or is good because of her surroundings. I will try her and find out.'

The following morning the maid did not appear before her mistress until nearly noon. The mistress was vexed and scolded her impatiently. The maid replied:

"If I am lazy for only a day or two, you ought not to become impatient." Then the mistress became angry.

The next day the maid got up late again. This made the mistress very angry and she struck the maid with a stick. This incident became widely known and the rich widow lost her good reputation.

3. Many people are like this woman. While their surroundings are satisfactory they are kind. Modest and quiet, but it is questionable if they will behave likewise when the conditions change and become unsatisfactory.

It is only when a person maintains a pure and peaceful mind and continues to act with goodness when unpleasant words enter his ears, when others show ill-will toward him or when he lacks sufficient food, clothes and shelter, that we may call him good.

Therefore, those who do good deeds and maintain a peaceful mind only when their surroundings are satisfactory are not really good people. Only those who have received the Buddha's teachings and are training their minds and bodies by those teachings can be called truly good, modest and peaceful people.

4. As to the suitability of words to be used there are five pairs of antonyms: words that are suitable to their occasions and those not so suitable to theirs; words that are beneficial and those that are harmful; and words that are sympathetic and those that are hateful.

Whatever words we utter should be chosen with care for people will hear them and be influenced by them for good or ill. If our minds are filled with sympathy and compassion, they will be resistant to the evil words we hear. We must not let wild words pass our lips lest they arouse feelings of anger and hatred. The words we speak should always be words of sympathy and wisdom.

Suppose there is a man who wants to remove all the dirt from the ground. He uses a spade and a window and works perseveringly scattering the dirt all about, but it is an impossible task. Like this foolish man we cannot hope to eliminate all words. We must train our mind and fill our hearts with sympathy so that we will be undisturbed by the words spoken by others.

One might try to paint a picture with water colours on the blue sky, but it is impossible. And it is also impossible to dry up a great river by the heat of a torch made of hay, or to produce a crackling noise by rubbing together two pieces of well-tanned leather. Like these examples, people should train their minds so that they would not be disturbed by whatever kinds of words they might hear.

They should train their minds and keep them broad as the earth, unlimited as the sky, deep as a big river and soft as well-tanned leather.

Even if your enemy catches and tortures you, if you feel resentment, you are not following the Buddha's teachings. Under every circumstance you should learn to think: "My mind is unshakeable. Words of hatred and anger shall not pass my lips. I will surround my enemy with thoughts of sympathy and pity that flow out from a mind filled with compassion for all sentient life."

5. There is a fable told of a man who found an anthill which burned in the daytime and smoked at night. He went to a wise man and asked his advice as to what he should do about it. The wise man told him to dig into it with a sword. This the man did. He found in succession a gate-bar, some bubbles of water, a pitchfork, a box, a tortoise, a butcher-knife, a piece of meat and, finally, a dragon which came out. The man reported to the wise man what he had found. The wise man explained the significance of it and said, "Throw away everything but the dragon; leave the dragon alone and do not disturb him."

This is a fable in which "anthill" represents the human body. "Burned in the daytime" represents the fact that during the day people turn into acts the things they thought about the previous night. "Smoked at night" indicates the fact that people during the night recall with pleasure or regret the things they did the previous day.

In the same fable, "a man" means a person who seeks Enlightenment. "A wise man" means Buddha. "A sword" means pure wisdom. "Dig into it" refers to the effort he must make to gain Enlightenment.

Further in the fable, "gate-bar" represents ignorance; "bubbles" are puffs of suffering and anger; "pitchfork" suggests hesitation and uneasiness; "box" suggests the storage of greed, anger, laziness, fickleness, repentance and delusion; "tortoise" means the body and the mind; "butcher-knife" means the synthesis of the five sensory desires, and "a piece of meat" means the resulting desire that causes a man to covet after satisfaction. These things are all harmful to man and so Buddha said, "Throw away everything."

Still further, "dragon" indicates a mind that has eliminated all worldly passions. If a man digs into things about him with the sword of wisdom he will finally come to his dragon. "Leave the dragon alone and do not disturb him" means to go after and dig up a mind free of worldly desires.

6. Pindola, a disciple of Buddha, after gaining Enlightenment, returned to his native place of Kausambi to repay the people there for the kindness they had shown him. In so doing he prepared the field for the sowing of Buddha-seeds.

On the outskirts of Kausambi there is a small park that runs along the bank of the Ganges River shaded by endless rows of coconut trees and where a cool wind continually blows.

One hot summer day, Pindola sat in meditation in the cool shade of a tree when King Udayana came to this park with his consorts for recreation and after that he took a nap in the shade of another tree.

While their king was asleep, his wives and ladies-in-waiting took a walk and suddenly came upon Pindola sitting in meditation. They recognised him as a holy-man and asked him to teach them, and they listened to his sermon.

When the king awoke from his nap, he went in search of his ladies and found them surrounding this man and listening to his teachings. Being of a jealous and lascivious mind, the king became angry and abused Pindola, saying: "It is inexcusable that you, a holy-man, should be in the midst of women and enjoy idle talk with them." Pindola quietly closed his eyes and remained silent.

The angry king drew his sword and threatened Pindola, but the holy-man remained silent and was as firm as a rock. This made the king still more angry so he broke open an anthill and threw some of the ant-filled dirt upon him, but still Pindola remained sitting in meditation, quietly enduring the insult and pain.

Thereupon, the king became ashamed of his ferocious conduct and begged Pindola's pardon. As a result of this incident, the Buddha's teachings found its way into the king's castle and from there it spread all over the country.

7. A few days Later King Udayana visited Pindola in the forest retreat where he lived and asked him, "Honoured teacher, how is it that the disciples of Buddha can keep their bodies and

minds pure and untempted by lust, although they are mostly young men?"

Pindola replied: "Noble Lord, Buddha has taught us to respect all women. He has taught us to look upon all old women as our mothers, upon those of our own age as our sisters, and upon younger ones as our daughters. Because of this teaching the disciples of Buddha are able to keep their bodies and minds pure and untempted by lust although are youthful."

"But, Honoured teacher, one may have impure thoughts of a woman the age of a mother or a sister or a daughter. How do the disciples of Buddha control their desires?"

"Noble Lord, the Blessed One taught us to think of our bodies as secreting impurities of all kinds such as blood, pus, sweat and oils; by thinking thus, we, although young, are able to keep our minds pure."

"Honoured teacher," still pressed the king. "It may be easy for you to do this for you have trained your body and mind, and polished your wisdom, but it would be difficult for those who have not yet had such training. Eyes will follow beautiful forms. They may try to see the ugliness but they will be tempted by the beautiful figures just the same. There must be some other reason that the young men among the Buddha's disciples are able to keep their actions pure."

"Noble Lord," replied Pindola, "the Blessed One teaches us to guard the doors of the five senses. When we see beautiful figures and colours with our eyes, when we hear pleasant sounds with our ears, when we smell fragrance with our nose, or when we taste sweet things with our tongue or touch soft things with our hands, we are not to become attached to these attractive things, neither are we to be repulsed by unattractive things. We are taught to carefully guard the doors of these five senses. It is by this teachings of the Blessed One that even young disciples are able to keep their minds and bodies pure."

"The teachings of Buddha is truly marvellous. From my own experience I know that if I confront anything beautiful or pleasing, without being on my guard, I am disturbed by the sense impressions. It is of vital importance that we be on guard at the door of the five senses, at all times to keep our deeds pure."

8. Whenever a person expresses the thought of his mind in action there is always a reaction that follows. If one abuses you, there is always a reaction that follows. If one abuses you, there is a temptation to answer back, or to be revenged. It is like spitting against the wind, it harms no one but oneself. It is like sweeping dust against the wind, it does not get rid of the dust but defiles oneself. Misfortune always dogs the steps of one who gives way to the desire for revenge.

9. It is a very good deed to cast away greed and to cherish a mind of charity. It is still better to keep one's mind intent on respecting the Noble Path.

One should get rid of a selfish mind and replace it with a mind that is earnest to help others. An act to make another happy inspires the other to make still another happy, and so happiness is born from such an act.

Thousands of candles can be lighted from a single candle, and the life of the candle will not be shortened. Happiness never decreases by being shared.

Those who seek Enlightenment must be careful of each of their steps. No matter how high one's aspiration may be, it must be attained step by step. The steps of the path to Enlightenment must be taken in our everyday life.

10. At the very beginning of the path to Enlightenment there are twenty difficulties for us to overcome in this world, and they are:
1. It is hard for a poor man to be generous.
2. It is hard for a proud *mana* to learn the Way of Enlightenment.
3. It is hard to seek Enlightenment at the cost of self-sacrifice.
4. It is hard to be born while Buddha is in the world.

5. It is hard to hear the teachings of Buddha.
6. It is hard to keep the mind pure against the instincts of the body.
7. It is hard not to desire things that are beautiful and attractive.
8. It is hard for a strong man not to use his strength to satisfy his desires.
9. It is hard not to get angry when one is insulted.
10. It is hard to remain innocent when tempted by sudden circumstances.
11. It is hard to apply oneself to study widely and thoroughly.
12. It is hard not to despise a beginner.
13. It is hard to keep oneself humble.
14. It is hard to find good friends.
15. It is hard to endure the discipline that leads to Enlightenment.
16. It is hard not to be disturbed by external conditions and circumstances.
17. It is hard to teach others by knowing their abilities.
18. It is hard to maintain a peaceful mind.
19. It is hard not to argue about right and wrong.
20. It is hard to find and learn a good method.

11. Good men and bad men differ from each other in their natures. Bad men do not recognise a sinful act as sinful; if its sinfulness is brought to their attention, they do not cease doing it and do not like to have anyone inform them of their sinful acts. Wise men are sensitive to right and wrong; they cease doing anything as soon as they see that it is wrong; they are grateful to anyone who calls their attention to such wrong acts.

Thus good men and bad men differ radically. Bad men never appreciate kindness shown to them, but wise men appreciate and are grateful. Wise men try to express their appreciation and gratitude by some return of kindness, not only to their benefactor, but to everyone else.

III

Teachings in Ancient Fables

1. Once upon a time there was a country which had the very peculiar custom of abandoning its aged people in remote and inaccessible mountains.

A certain minister of the State found it too difficult to follow this custom in the case of his own aged father, and so he built a secret underground cave where he hid his father and cared for him.

One day a god appeared before the king of that country and gave him a puzzling problem, saying that if he could not solve it satisfactorily, his country would be destroyed. The problem was: "Here are two serpents; tell me the sex of each."

Neither the king nor anyone in the palace was able to solve the problem; so the king offered a great reward to anyone in his kingdom who could.

The minister went to his father's hiding place and asked him for the answer to that problem. The old man said: "It is an easy solution. Place the two snakes on a soft carpet; the one that moves about is the male, and the other that keeps quiet is the female." The minister carried the answer to the king and the problem was successfully solved.

Then the god asked other difficult questions which the king and his retainers were unable to answer, but which the minister, after consulting his aged father, could always solve.

Here are some of the questions and their answers. "Who is the one who, being asleep, is called the awakened one, and, being awake, is called the sleeping one?" The answer to this is: It is the one who is under training for Enlightenment. He is awake when compared with those who are not interested in Enlightenment; he is asleep when compared with those who have already attained Enlightenment.

"How can you weigh a large elephant?" "Load it on a boat and draw a line to mark how deep the boat sinks into the water. Then take out the elephant and load the boat with stones until it sinks to the same depth, and then weigh the stones."

What is the meaning of the saying, "A cupful of water is more than the water of an ocean?" This is the answer: "A cupful of water given in a pure and compassionate spirit to one's parents or to a sick person has an eternal merit, but the water of an ocean will some day come to an end."

Next the god made a starving man, reduced to skin and bones, complain, "Is there anyone in this world more hungry than I?" "The man who is so selfish and greedy that he does not believe in the Three Treasures of the Buddha, the Dharma and the Samgha, and who does not make offerings to his parents and teachers, is not only more hungry but he will fall into the world of hungry demons and there he will suffer from hunger forever?"

"Here is a plank of Chandana (sandalwood); which end was the bottom of the tree?" "Float the plank in water; the end that sinks a little deeper was the end nearest the root."

"Here are two horses apparently of the same size and form; how can you tell mother from the son?" "Feed them some hay; the mother horse will push the hay toward her son."

Every answer to these difficult questions pleased the god as well as the king. The king was grateful to find out that the answers had come from the aged father whom the minister had hidden in the cave, and he withdrew the law of abandoning aged people in the mountains and ordered that they were to be treated kindly.

2. Queen of Videha in India once dreamed of a white elephant that had six ivory tusks. She coveted the tusks and besought the king to get them for her. Although the task seemed an impossible one, the king who loved the queen very much offered a reward to any hunter who would report if he found such an elephant.

It happened that there was just such an elephant with six tusks in the Himalayan Mountains who was training for Buddhahood. The elephant once had saved a hunter's life in an emergency in the depths of the mountains as a result of which the hunter could go back safely to his country. The hunter, however, blinded by the great reward and forgetting the kindness the elephant had shown him, returned to the mountains to kill the elephant.

The hunter, knowing that the elephant was seeking Buddhahood, disguised himself in the robe of a Buddhist monk and, thus catching the elephant off guard, shot it with a poisoned arrow.

The elephant, knowing that its end was near and that the hunter had been overcome by the worldly desire for the reward, had compassion upon him and sheltered him in its limbs to protect the hunter from the fury of the other revengeful elephants. Then the elephant asked the hunter why he had done such a foolish thing. The hunter told of the reward and confessed that he coveted its six tusks. The elephant immediately broke off the tusks by hitting them against a tree and gave them to the hunter saying: "By this offering I have completed my training for Buddhahood and will be reborn in the Pure Land. When I become a Buddha, I will help you to get rid of your three poisonous arrows of greed, anger and foolishness."

3. In a thicket at the foot of the Himalayan Mountains there once lived a parrot together with many other animals and birds. One day a fire started in the thicket from the friction of bamboos in a strong wind and the birds and animals were frightened and confused. The parrot, feeling compassion for their fright and suffering and wishing to repay the kindness he had received in the bamboo thicket where he could shelter himself, tried to do all he could to save them. He dipped himself in a pond nearby and flew over the fire and shook off the drops of water to extinguish the fire. He repeated this diligently with a heart of compassion out of gratitude to the thicket.

This spirit of kindness and self-sacrifice was noticed by a heavenly god who came down from the sky and said to the parrot: "You have a gallant mind, but what good do you expect to accomplish by a few drops of water against this great fire?" The parrot answered: "There is nothing that cannot be accomplished by the spirit of gratitude and self-sacrifice. I will try over and over again and then over in the next life." The great god was impressed by the parrot's spirit and together they extinguished the fire.

4. At one time there lived in the Himalayas a bird with one body and two heads. Once one of the heads noticed the other head eating some sweet fruit and felt jealous and said to itself: "I will then eat poison fruit." So it ate poison and the whole bird died.

5. At one time the tail and the head of a snake quarrelled as to which should be the front. The tail said to the head: "You are always taking the lead; it is not fair, you ought to let me lead sometimes." The head answered: "It is the law of our nature that I should be the head; I cannot change places with you."

But the quarrel went on and one day the tail fastened itself to a tree and thus prevented the head from proceeding. When the head became tired with the struggle the tail had its own way, with the result that the snake fell into a pit of fire and perished.

In the world of nature there always exists an appropriate order and everything has its own function. If this order is disturbed, the functioning is interrupted and the whole order will go to ruin.

6. There was a man who was easily angered. One day two men were talking in front of the house about the man who lived there. One said to the other: "He is a nice man but is very impatient; he has a hot temper and gets angry quickly." The man overheard the remark, rushed out of the house and attacked the two men, striking and kicking and wounding them. When a wise man is advised of his errors, he will reflect

on them and improve his conduct. When his misconduct is pointed out, a foolish man will not only disregard the advice but rather repeat the same error.

7. Once there was a wealthy but foolish man. When he saw the beautiful three-storeyed house of another man, he envied it and made up his mind to have one built just like it, thinking he was himself just as wealthy. He called a carpenter and ordered him to build it. The carpenter consented and immediately began to construct the foundation, the first story, the second story, and then the third story. The wealthy man noticed this with irritation and said: "I don't want a foundation or a first story or a second story; I just want the beautiful third story. Build it quickly.

A foolish man always thinks only of the results, and is impatient without the effort that is necessary to get good results. No good can be attained without proper effort, just as there can be no third story without the foundation and the first and the second stories.

8. A foolish man was once boiling honey. His friend suddenly appeared and the foolish man wanted to offer him some honey, but it was too hot, and so without removing it from the fire he fanned it to make it cool. In like manner, it is impossible to get the honey of cool wisdom without first removing it from the fire of worldly passions.

9. Once there were two demons who spent a whole day arguing and quarrelling about a box, a cane and a pair of shoes. A man, passing by, inquired, "Why are you arguing about these things? What magical power do they have that you should be quarrelling about possessing them?"

The demons explained to him that from the box they could get anything they desired – food, clothing or treasure; with the cane they could subdue all their enemies; and with the pair of shoes they could travel through the air.

Upon hearing this, the man said: "Why quarrel? If you will go away for a few minutes, I can think of a fair division of the things between you." So the two demons retired and a soon as they were gone, the man put on the shoes, seized the box and the cane and was off through the air.

The "demons" represent men of heathen beliefs. "A box" means the gifts that are made in charity; they do not realise how many treasures can be produced from charity. "A cane" means the practice of concentration of the mind. Men do not realise that by the practice of spiritual concentration of mind, they can subdue all worldly desires. "A pair of shoes" means the pure disciplines of thought and conduct, that will carry them beyond all desires and arguments. Without knowing these, they quarrel and argue about a box, a cane and a pair of shoes.

10. Once upon a time a man was travelling alone. He came to a vacant house towards the evening and decided to spend the night there. About midnight a demon brought in a corpse and left it on the floor. Shortly, another demon appeared and claimed the corpse as his and they quarrelled over it.

Then the first demon said it was useless to argue about it further and proposed that they refer it to a judge to decide the possessor. The other demon agreed to this and, seeing the man cowering in the corner, asked him to decide the ownership. The man was terribly frightened, for he well knew that whatever decision he might make would anger the demon that lost and that the losing demon would seek revenge and kill him, but he decided to tell truthfully just what he had witnessed.

As he expected, this angered the second demon who grabbed one of the man's arms and tore it off, but the first demon replaced the arm with the one taken from the corpse. The angry demon tore away the man's other arm, but the first demon immediately replaced the other arm of the corpse. And so it went on until both arms, both legs, the head and the body had been successively torn away and replaced with the corresponding parts of the corpse. Then the two demons, seeing the parts of the man scattered about on the floor, picked them up and devoured them and went away chuckling.

The poor man who had taken refuge in the deserted house was very much upset by his misfortunes. The parts of his body which the demons had eaten were the parts his parents had given him, and the parts that he now had belonged to the corpse. Who was he, anyway? Realising all the facts, he was unable to figure it out, and becoming crazy, he wandered out of the house. Coming to a temple, he went in and told his troubles to the monks. People could see the true meaning of selflessness in his story.

11. Once a beautiful and well-dressed woman visited a house. The master of the house asked her who she was; and she replied that she was the goddess of wealth. The master of the house was delighted and so treated her nicely.

Soon after another woman appeared who was ugly looking and poorly dressed. The master asked who she was and the woman replied that she was the goddess of poverty. The master was frightened and tried to drive her out of the house, but the woman refused to depart, saying, "The goddess of wealth is my sister. There is an agreement between us that we are never to live separately; if you chase me out, she is to go with me." Sure enough, as soon as the ugly woman went out, the other woman disappeared.

Birth goes with death. Fortune goes with misfortune. Bad things follow good things. Men should realise this. Foolish people dread misfortune and strive after good fortune, but those who seek Enlightenment must transcend both of them and be free of worldly attachments.

12. Once there lived a poor artist who left his home, leaving his wife, to seek his fortune. After three years of hard struggles he had saved three hundred pieces of gold to return to his home. On his way he came to a great temple in which a grand

ceremony of offering was in progress. He was greatly impressed by it and thought to himself: 'Hitherto, I have thought only of the present; I have never considered my future happiness. It is a part of my good fortune that I have come to this place; I must take advantage of it to plant seeds of merit.' Thinking thus, he gratefully donated all his savings to the temple and returned to his home penniless.

When he reached home, his wife reproached him for not bringing her some money for her support. The poor artist replied that he had earned some money but had put it where it would be safe. When she pressed him to tell where he had hidden it, he confessed that he had given it to the monks at a certain temple.

This made the wife angry and she scolded her husband and finally carried the matter to the local judge. When the judge asked the artist for his defence, the artist said that he had not acted foolishly, for he had earned the money during long and hard struggles and wanted to use it as seed for future good fortune. When he came to the temple it seemed to him that there was the field where he should plant his gold as seed for good fortune. Then he added: "When I gave the monks the gold, it seemed that I was throwing away all greed and stinginess from my mind, and I have realised that real wealth is not gold but mind."

The judge praised the artist's spirit, and those who heard of this manifested their approval by helping him in various ways. Thus the artist and his wife entered into permanent good fortune.

13. A man living near a cemetery heard one night a voice calling him from a grave. He was too timid to investigate it himself but the next day he mentioned it to a brave friend, who made up his mind to trace the place whence the voice came the following night.

While the timid man was trembling with fear, his friend went to the cemetery and, sure enough, it was the same voice. When asked what it wanted, the voice from under the ground replied: "I am a hidden treasure that has decided to give myself to someone. I offered it to a man last night but he was too timid to come after it, so I will give it to you who are worthy of it. Tomorrow morning I will come to your house with my seven followers."

The friend said: "I will be waiting for you, but please tell me how I am to treat you." The voice replied: "We will come in monk's robes. Have a room ready for us with water; wash your body and clean the room, and have seats for us and eight bowls of rice-porridge. After the meal, you are to lead us one by one into a closed room in which we will transform ourselves into crocks of gold."

The next morning this man washed his body and cleaned the room just as he had been told and waited for the eight monks to appear. In due time they appeared and he received them courteously. After they had eaten the food he led them one by one into the closed room, where each monk turned himself into a crock full of gold.

There was a very greedy man in the same village who learned of the incident and wanted the crocks of gold. He invited eight monks to his house. After their meal he led them into a closed room, but instead of turning themselves into crocks of gold, they became angry and rough and reported the greedy man to the police who eventually arrested him.

As for the timid man, when he heard that the voice from the grave had brought wealth to the brave man, he went to the house of the brave man and greedily demanded the gold, insisting that it was his, because the voice first addressed him. When the timid man tried to take the crocks away he found lots of snakes inside raising their heads ready to attack him.

The king heard about this and ruled that the crocks belonged to the brave man and uttered the following observation: "Everything in the world goes like this. Foolish people are avaricious for good results only, but are too timid to go after them and, therefore, are continually failing. They have neither faith nor courage to face the internal struggles of the mind by which alone true peace and harmony can be attained."

Chapter Two

The Way of Practical Attainment

I

Search for Truth

1. In the search for truth there are certain questions that are unimportant. Of what material is the universe constructed? Is the universe eternal? Are there limits to the universe or not ? In what way is this human society put together? What is the ideal form of organisation for human society? If a man were to postpone his search and practice for Enlightenment until such questions were solved, he would die before he found the path.

Suppose a man were pierced by a poisoned arrow, and his relatives and friends got together to call a surgeon to have the arrow pulled out and the wound treated.

If the wounded man objects, saying, "Wait a little. Before you pull it out, I want to know who shot this arrow. Was it a man or a woman? Was it someone of noble birth, or was it a peasant? What was the bow made of? Was it a big bow, or a small bow, that shot the arrow? Was it made of wood or bamboo? What was the bowstring made of? Was it made of fibre, or of gut? Was the arrow made of rattan, or of reed? What feathers were used? Before you extract the arrow, I want to know all about these things." Then what will happen?

Before all this information can be secured, no doubt, the poison will have time to circulate all through the system and the man may die. The first duty is to remove the arrow, and prevent its poison from spreading.

When a fire of passion is endangering the world, the composition of the universe matters little; what is the ideal form for the human community is not so important to deal with.

The question of whether the universe has limits or is eternal can wait until some way is found to extinguish the fires of birth, old age, sickness and death; in the presence of misery, sorrow, suffering and agony, one should first search for a way to solve these problems and devote oneself to the practice of that way.

The Buddha's teachings contains what is important to know and not what is unimportant. That is, it teaches people that they must learn what they should learn, remove what they should remove, train for what they should become enlightened about.

Therefore, people should first discern what is the most important, what problem should be solved first and what is the most pressing issue for them. To do all this, they must first undertake to train their minds; that is, they must first seek mind-control.

2. Suppose a man goes to the forest to get some of the pith that grows in the centre of a tree and returns with a burden of branches and leaves, thinking that he has secured what he went after; would he not be foolish, if he is satisfied with the bark, wood for the pith which he was after? But that is what many people are doing.

A person seeks a path that will lead away from birth, old age, sickness and death, or from misery, sorrow, suffering and agony; and yet, he follows the path a little way, notices some little advance, and immediately becomes proud and conceited and domineering. He is like the man who sought pith and went away satisfied with a burden of branches and leaves.

Another man becoming satisfied with the progress he has made by a little effort, relaxes his effort and becomes proud and conceited; he is carrying away only a load of branches instead of the pith he was seeking.

Then again, another man becomes proud and conceited because he notices that he had gained a measure of intuitive insight; he has a load of the wood fibre of the tree instead of the pith. All of these seekers, who become easily satisfied by their insufficient effort and become proud and overbearing, relax their efforts and easily fall into idleness. All these people will inevitably face suffering again.

Those who seek the true path to Enlightenment must not expect any offer of respect, honour or devotion. And further, they must not aim with a slight effort, at a trifling advance in calmness or knowledge or insight.

First of all, one should get clearly in mind the basic and essential nature of this world of life and death.

3. The world has no substance of its own. It is simply a vast concordance of causes and conditions that have had their origin, solely and exclusively, in the activities of the mind that has been stimulated by ignorance, false imagination, desires and infatuation. It is not something external about which the mind has false conceptions; it has no substance whatever. It has come into appearance by the processes of the mind itself, manifesting its own delusions. It is founded and built up out of the desires of the mind, out of its sufferings and struggles incidental to the pain cause by its own greed, anger and foolishness. Men who seek the way to Enlightenment should be ready to fight such a mind to attain their goal.

4. "Oh my mind! Why do you hover so restlessly over the changing circumstances of life? Why do you make me so confused and restless? Why do you urge me to collect so many things? You are like a plow that breaks in pieces before beginning to plow; you are like a rudder that is dismantled just as you are venturing out on the sea of life and death. Of What use are many rebirths if we do not make good use of this life?

"Oh my mind! Once you caused me to be born as a king, and then you caused me to be born as an outcast and to beg for my food. Sometimes you cause me to be born in heavenly mansions of the gods and to dwell in luxury and in ecstasy; then you plunge me into the flames of hell.

"Oh, my foolish, foolish mind! Thus you have led me along different paths and I have been obedient to you and docile. But now that I have heard the Buddha's teachings, do not disturb me any more or cause me further sufferings, but let us seek Enlightenment together, humbly and patiently.

"Oh, my mind! If you could only learn that everything is non-substantial and transitory; if you could only learn not to grasp after things, not to covet things, not to give way to greed, anger and foolishness; then we might journey in quietness. Then, by severing the bond of desires with the sword of wisdom, being undisturbed by changing circumstances – advantage or disadvantage, good or bad, loss or gain, praise or abuse – we might dwell in peace.

"Oh, my dear mind! Why do you rush hither and thither with no definite purpose? Let us cross this wild sea of delusion. Hitherto I have actèd as you wished, but now you must act as I wish and, together, we will follow the Buddha's teachings.

"Oh, my dear mind! These mountains, rivers and seas are changeable and cause pain. Where in this world of delusion shall we seek quietness? Let us follow the Buddha's teachings and cross over to the other shore of Enlightenment."

5. Thus, those who really seek the path to Enlightenment dictate terms to their mind. Then they proceed with strong determination. Even though they are abused by some and scorned by others, they go forward undisturbed. They do not become angry if they are beaten by fists, or hit by stones, or gashed by swords.

Even if enemies cut their head from the body, the mind must not be disturbed. If they let their mind become darkened by the things they suffer, they are not following the teachings of Buddha. They must be determined, no matter what happens to them, to remain steadfast, unmovable, ever radiating thoughts of compassion and goodwill. Let abuse come, let misfortune come, and yet one should resolve to remain unmoved and tranquil in mind, filled with Buddha's teachings.

For the sake of attaining Enlightenment, one should try to accomplish the impossible and one should endure the unendurable. One must give what he has to the last of it. If he is told that to gain Enlightenment he must limit his food to a single grain of rice a day, he will eat only that. If the path to Enlightenment leads him through fire, he will go forward.

But one must not do these things for any ulterior purpose. One should do them because it is the wise thing, the right thing, to do. One should do them out of a spirit of compassion, as a mother does things for her little child, for her sick child, with no thought of her own strength or comfort.

6. Once there was a king who loved his people and his country and ruled them with wisdom and kindness, and because of it his country was prosperous and peaceful. He was always seeking for greater wisdom and Enlightenment; he even offered rewards to anyone who could lead him to worthy teachings.

His devotion and wisdom finally came to the attention of the gods, but they determined to test him. A god in disguise as a demon appeared before the gates of the king's place and asked to be brought before the king as he had a holy teaching to share with him.

The king who was pleased to hear the message courteously received him and asked for instruction. The demon took on a dreadful form and demanded food, saying that he could not teach until he had the food he liked. Choice food was offered to the demon, but he insisted that he must have warm human flesh and blood. The crown-prince gave his body and the queen also gave her body, but still the demon was unsatisfied and so demanded the body of the king.

The king expressed his willingness to give his body, but asked that he might first hear the teaching before he would offer his body.

The god uttered the following wise teaching: "Misery rises from lust and fear rises from lust. Those who remove lust have no misery or fear." Suddenly the god resumed his true form and the prince and the queen also reappeared in their original bodies.

7. Once there was a person who sought the True Path in the Himalayas. He cared nothing for all the treasures of the earth or even for all the delights of heaven, but he sought the teaching that would remove all mental delusions.

The gods were impressed by the man's earnestness and sincerity and decided to test his mind. So one of the gods disguised himself as a demon and appeared in the Himalayas, singing: "Everything changes, everything appears and disappears."

The seeker heard this song which pleased him very much. He was as delighted as if he had found a spring of cool water for his thirst or as if a slave had been unexpectedly set free. He said to himself, "At last I have found the true teaching that I have sought for so long." He followed the voice and at last came upon the frightful demon. With an uneasy mind he approached the demon and said: "Was it you who sang the holy song that I have just heard? If it was you, please sing more of it."

The demon replied: "Yes, it was my song, but I cannot sing more of it until I have had something to eat; I am starving."

The man begged him very earnestly to sing more of it, saying: "It has a sacred meaning to me and I have sought its teaching for a long time. I have only heard a part of it; please let me hear more."

The demon said again: "I am starving, but if I can taste the warm flesh and blood of a man, I will finish the song."

The man, in his eagerness to hear the teaching, promised the demon that he could have his body after he had heard the teaching. The demon sang the complete song.

Everything changes,
Everything appears and disappears,
There is perfect tranquillity
When one transcends both life and extinction.

Hearing this, the man, after he wrote the poem on rocks
and trees around, quietly climbed a tree and hurled himself to
the feet of the demon, but the demon had disappeared and,
instead, a radiant god received the body of the man unharmed.

8.   Once upon a time there was an earnest seeker of the true
path named Sadaprarudita. He cast aside every temptation for
profit or honour and sought the path at the risk of his life. One
day a voice from heaven came to him, saying, "Sadaprarudita!
Go straight toward the east. Do not think of either heat or cold,
pay no attention to worldly praise or scorn, do not be bothered
by discriminations of good or evil, but just keep on going east.
In the far east you will find a true teacher and will gain
Enlightenment."

Sadaprarudita was very pleased to get this definite
instruction and immediately started on his journey eastward.
Sometimes he slept where night found him in a lonely field or
in the wild mountains.

Being a stranger in foreign lands, he suffered many
humiliations; once he sold himself into slavery, selling his own
flesh out of hunger, but at last he found the true teacher and
asked for his instruction.

There is a saying, "Good things are costly," and
Sadaprarudita found it true in his case, for he had many
difficulties on his journey in search of the path. He had no
money to buy some flowers and incense to offer the teacher.
He tried to sell his services but could find no one to hire him.
There seemed to be an evil spirit hindering him every way he
turned. The path to Enlightenment is a hard one and it may
cost a man his life.

At last Sadaprarudita reached the presence of the teacher
himself and then he had a new difficulty. He had no paper on
which to take notes and no brush or ink to write with. Then he

pricked his wrist with a dagger and took notes in his own blood. In this way he secured the precious Truth.

9. Once there was a boy named Sudhana who also wished for Enlightenment and earnestly sought the way. From a fisherman he learned the lore of the sea. From a doctor he learned compassion toward sick people in their suffering. From a wealthy man he learned that saving pennies was the secret of his fortune and thought how necessary it was to conserve every trifling gained on the path to Enlightenment.

From a meditating monk he learned that the pure and peaceful mind had a miraculous power to purify and tranquillise other minds. Once he met a woman of exceptional personality and was impressed by her benevolent spirit, and from her he learned a lesson that charity was the fruit of wisdom. Once he met an aged wanderer who told him that to reach a certain place he had to scale a mountain of swords and pass through a valley of fire. Thus Sudhana learned from his experiences that there was true teaching to be gained from everything he saw or heard.

He learned patience from a poor, crippled woman; he learned a lesson of simple happiness from watching children playing in the street; and from some gentle and humble people, who never thought of wanting anything that anybody else wanted, he learned the secret of living at peace with all the world.

He learned a lesson of harmony from watching the blending of the elements of incense, and a lesson of thanksgiving from the arrangement of flowers. One day, passing through a forest, he took a rest under a noble tree and noticed a tiny seedling growing nearby out of a fallen and decaying tree and it taught him a lesson of the uncertainty of life.

Sunlight by day and the twinkling stars by night constantly refreshed his spirit. Thus Sudhana profited by the experiences of his long journey.

Indeed, those who seek for Enlightenment must think of their minds as castles and decorate them. They must open wide the gates of their minds for Buddha, and respectfully and humbly invite Him to enter the innermost chamber, there to offer Him the fragrant incense of faith and the flowers of gratitude and gladness.

II
The Ways of Practice

1. For those who seek Enlightenment there are three ways of practice that must be understood and followed: First, disciplines for practical behaviour; second, right concentration of mind; and third, wisdom.

What are disciplines? Everyone, whether he is a common man or a way-seeker, should follow the precepts for good behaviour. He should control both his mind and body, and guard the gates of his five senses. He should be afraid of even a trifling evil and, from moment to moment, should endeavour to practise only good deeds.

What is meant by the concentration of mind? It means to get quickly away from greedy and evil desires as they arise and to hold the mind pure and tranquil.

What is wisdom? It is the ability to perfectly understand and to patiently accept the Fourfold Noble Truth, to know the fact of suffering and its nature; to know the source of suffering, to know what constitutes the end of suffering, and to know the Noble Path that leads to the end of suffering.

Suppose a donkey, that has no nice shape, no voice and no horns like those of the cow, was following a herd of cows and proclaiming, "Look, I am also a cow." Would any one believe him? It is just as foolish when a man does not follow the three ways of practice but boasts that he is a way-seeker or a disciple of Buddha.

Before a farmer gathers a harvest in the fall, he must first plow the ground, sow the seed, irrigate, and remove the weeds as they come up in the springtime. Likewise, the seeker of

Enlightenment must follow the three ways of practice. A farmer cannot expect to see the buds today, to see the plants tomorrow, and to gather the harvest the day after. So a man who seeks Enlightenment cannot expect to remove worldly desires today, to remove attachments and evil desires tomorrow, and to get Enlightenment the day after.

Just as plants receive the patient care of the farmer after the seed has been sown and during the changes of climate and during the growth from plant to fruit, so the seeker of Enlightenment must patiently and perseveringly cultivate the soil of Enlightenment by following the three ways of practice.

2. It is difficult to advance along the path that leads to Enlightenment so long as one is covetous of comforts and luxuries and his mind is disturbed by the desires of the senses. There is a wide difference between the enjoyment of life and the enjoyment of the True Path.

As already explained, the mind is the source of all things. If the mind enjoys worldly affairs, illusions and suffering will inevitably follow, but if the mind enjoys the True Path, happiness, contentment and Enlightenment will just as surely follow.

Therefore, those who are seeking Enlightenment should keep their minds pure, and patiently keep and practise the three ways. If they keep the precepts they will naturally obtain concentration of mind; and if they obtain concentration of the mind it will be just as natural for them to grasp wisdom which will lead them to Enlightenment.

Indeed, these three ways (keeping the precepts, practising concentration of mind and always acting wisely) are the true path to Enlightenment.

By not following them, people have for a long time accumulated mental delusions. They must not argue with worldly people, but must patiently meditate in their inner world of a pure mind in order to attain Enlightenment.

3. If the three ways of practice are analysed, they will reveal the Noble Eightfold Path, the four viewpoints to be considered, the four right procedures, the five faculties of power to be employed, and the perfection of six practices.

The Noble Eightfold Path refers to right view, right thought, right speech, right behaviour, right livelihood, right effort, right mindfulness, and right concentration.

Right View means to thoroughly understand the Fourfold Truth, to believe in the law of cause and effect and not to be deceived by appearances and desires.

Right Thought means the resolution not to cherish desires, not to be greedy, not to be angry, and not to do any harmful deed.

Right Speech means the avoidance of lying words, idle words, abusive words, and double-tongues.

Right Behaviour means not to destroy any life, not to steal or not to commit adultery.

Right Livelihood means to avoid any life that would bring shame.

Right Effort means to try to do one's best diligently toward the right direction.

Right Mindfulness means to maintain a pure and thoughtful mind.

Right Concentration means to keep the mind right and tranquil for its concentration, seeking to realise the mind's pure essence.

4. The four viewpoints to be considered are: first, to consider the body impure, seeking to remove all attachment to it, second, to consider the senses as a source of suffering, whatever their feelings of pain or pleasure may be; third, to consider the mind to be in a constant state of flux, and fourth, to consider everything in the world as being a consequence of causes and conditions and that nothing remains unchanged forever.

5. The four right procedures are: first, to prevent any evil from starting; second, to remove any evil as soon as it starts; third, to induce the doing of good deed; and fourth, to encourage the growth and continuance of good deeds that have already started. One must endeavour to keep these four procedures.

6. The five faculties of power are: first, the faith to believe; second, the will to make the endeavour; third, the faculty of alertness; fourth, the ability to concentrate one's mind; and fifth, the ability to maintain clear wisdom. These five faculties are necessary powers to attain Enlightenment.

7. The perfection of six practices for reaching the other shore of Enlightenment are: the path of offering, the path of keeping precepts, the path of endurance, the path of endeavour, the path of concentration of mind, and the path of wisdom. By following these paths, one can surely pass from the shore of delusion over to the shore of Enlightenment.

The practice of Offering gets rid of selfishness; the practice of Precepts keeps one thoughtful of the rights and comforts of others; the practice of Endurance helps one to control a fearful or angry mind; the practice of Endeavour helps one to be diligent and faithful; the practice of Concentration helps one to control a wandering and futile mind; and the practice of Wisdom changes a dark and confused mind into a clear and penetrating insight.

Offering and keeping Precepts make the necessary foundation to build a great castle on. Endurance and Endeavour are the walls of the castle that protect it against enemies from outside. Concentration and Wisdom are the personal armour that protects one against the assaults of life and death.

If one gives away a gift only when convenient, or because it is easier to give than not to give, it is an offering, of course, but it is not a True Offering. A True Offering comes from a sympathetic heart before any request is made, and a True Offering is the one that gives not occasionally but constantly.

Neither is it a True Offering if after the act there are feelings of regret or of self-praise; a True Offering is one that is given with pleasure, forgetting oneself as the giver, the one who receives it and the gift itself.

True Offering springs spontaneously from one's pure compassionate heart with no thought of any return, wishing to enter into a life of Enlightenment together.

There are seven kinds of offering which can be practised by even those who are not wealthy. The first is the physical offering. This is to offer service by one's labour. The highest type of this offering is to offer one's ówn life as is shown in the following story. The second is the spiritual offering. This is to offer a compassionate heart to others. The third is the offering of eyes. This is to offer a warm glance to others which will give them tranquillity. The fourth is the offering of countenance. This is to offer a soft countenance with smile to others. The fifth is the oral offering. This is to offer kind and warm words to others. The sixth is the seat offering. This is to offer one's seat to others. The seventh is the offering of shelter. This is to let others spend the night at one's home. These kinds of offering can be practised by anyone in everyday life.

8.   Once there was a prince named Sattva. One day he and his two elder brothers went to a forest to play. There they saw a famished tigress which was evidently tempted to devour her own seven cubs to satisfy her hunger.

The elder brother ran away in fear but Satta climbed up a cliff and threw himself over the tigress in order to save the lives of the baby tigers.

Prince Sattva did this charitable act spontaneously but within his mind he was thinking: "This body is changing and impermanent; I have loved this body with no thought of throwing it away, but now I make it an offering to this tigress so that I may gain Enlightenment." This thought of prince Sattva shows the true determination to gain Enlightenment.

9. There are Four Unlimited States of Mind that the seeker of Enlightenment should cherish. They are compassion, tenderness, gladness and equanimity. One can remove greed by cherishing compassion; one can remove anger by tenderness; one can remove suffering by gladness, and one can remove the habit of discrimination of enemies and friends by cherishing an equitable mind.

It is a great compassion that makes people happy and contented; it is a great tenderness that removes everything that does not make people happy and contented; it is a great gladness that makes everyone happy and contented with a mind of joy; there is a great peacefulness when everyone is happy and contented, and then one can have equal feelings toward everybody.

With care one may cherish these Four Unlimited States of Mind and may get rid of greed, anger, suffering, and the minds of love-hate, but it is not an easy thing to do. An evil mind is as hard to get rid of as a watchdog, and a right mind is as easy to lose as a deer in a forest; or an evil mind is as hard to remove as letters carved in stone, and a right mind is as easy to lose as words written in water. Indeed, it is the most difficult thing in life to train oneself for Enlightenment.

10. There was a young man named Srona who was born in a wealthy·family but was of delicate health. He was very earnest to gain Enlightenment and became a disciple of the Blessed One. On the path to Enlightenment, he tried so hard that finally his feet bled.

The Blessed One pitied him and said, "Srona my boy, did you ever study the harp at your home? You know that a harp does not make music if the strings are stretched too tight or too loose. It makes music only when the strings are stretched just right.

"The training for Enlightenment is just like adjusting the harp strings. You cannot attain Enlightenment if you stretch the strings of your mind too loosely or too tightly. You must be considerate and act wisely."

Srona found these words very profitable and finally gained what he sought.

11. Once there was a prince who was skilful in the use of the five weapons. One day he was returning home from his practice and met a monster whose skin was invulnerable.

The monster started for him but nothing daunted the prince. He shot an arrow at him which fell harmless. Then he threw his spear which failed to penetrate the thick skin. Then he threw a bar and a javelin but they failed to hurt the monster. Then he used his sword but the sword broke. The prince attacked the monster with his fists and feet but to no purpose, for the monster clutched him in his giant arms and held him fast. Then the prince tried to use his head as a weapon but in vain.

The monster said, "It is useless for you to resist; I am going to devour you." But the prince answered, "You may think that I have used all my weapons and am helpless, but I still have one weapon left. If you devour me, I will destroy you from the inside of your stomach."

The courage of the prince disturbed the monster and he asked, "How can you do that?" The prince replied, "By the power of the Truth."

Then the monster released him and begged for his instruction in the Truth.

The teaching of this fable is to encourage disciples to persevere in their efforts and to be undaunted in the face of many setbacks.

12. Both odious self-assertion and shamelessness offend mankind, but dishonour and shame protect human beings. People respect their parents, elders, brothers and sisters because they are sensitive to dishonour and shame. After self-reflection it is meritorious to withhold honour from one's self and to feel ashamed by observing other people.

If a man possesses a repentant spirit his sins will disappear, but if he has an unrepentant spirit his sins will continue and condemn him forever.

It is only the one who hears the true teaching rightly and realises its meaning and relation to oneself who can receive and profit by it.

If a man merely hears the true teaching but does not acquire it, he will fail in his search for Enlightenment.

Faith, modesty, humbleness, endeavour and wisdom are the great sources of strength to him who is seeking Enlightenment. Among these, wisdom is the greatest of all and the rest are but the aspects of wisdom. If a man, while in his training, loves worldly affairs, enjoys idle talk or falls asleep, he will be retired from the path to Enlightenment.

13. In training for Enlightenment, some may succeed quicker than others. Therefore, one should not be discouraged to see others becoming enlightened first.

When a man is practising archery, he does not expect quick success but knows that if he practices patiently, he will become more and more accurate. A river begins as a brook but grows ever larger until it flows into the great ocean.

Like these examples, if a man trains with patience and perseverance, he will surely gain Enlightenment.

As already explained, if one keeps his eyes open, he will see the teaching everywhere, and so his opportunities for Enlightenment are endless.

Once there was a man who was burning incense. He noticed that the fragrance was neither coming nor going; it neither appeared nor disappeared. This trifle incident led him to gain Enlightenment.

Once there was a man who got a thorn stuck in his foot. He felt the sharp pain and a thought came to him, that pain was only a reaction of the mind. From this incident a deeper thought followed that the mind may get out of hand if one succeeds. From these thoughts, a little later, Enlightenment came to him.

There was another man who was very avaricious. One day
he was thinking of his greedy mind when he realised that
greedy thoughts were but shavings and kindlings that wisdom
could burn and consume. That was the beginning of his
Enlightenment.

There is an old saying: "Keep your mind level. If the mind
is level, the whole world will be level." Consider these words,
Realise that all the distinctions of the world are caused by the
discriminating views of the mind. There is a path to
Enlightenment in those very words. Indeed, the ways to
Enlightenment are unlimited.

III

The Way of Faith

1. Those who take refuge in the three treasures, the Buddha,
the Dharma and the Samgha, are called the disciples of
Buddha. The disciples of Buddha observe the four parts of
mind-control – the precepts, faith, offering and wisdom.

The disciples of Buddha practise the five precepts: not to
kill, not to steal, not to commit adultery, not to lie, and not to
take intoxicants of any kind.

The disciples of Buddha have faith in the Buddha's perfect
wisdom. They try to keep away from greediness and
selfishness and to practise offering. They understand the law
of cause and effect, keeping in mind the transiency of life and
conform to the norm of wisdom.

A tree leaning toward the east will naturally fall eastward
and so those who listen to the Buddha's teachings and maintain
faith in it will surely be born in the Buddha's Pure Land.

2. It has rightly been said that those who believe in the three
treasures of the Buddha, the Dharma and the Samgha are
called the disciples of Buddha.

The Buddha is the one who attained perfect Enlightenment
and used His attainment to emancipate and bless all mankind.
The Dharma is the truth, the spirit of Enlightenment and the

teaching that explains it. The Samgha is the perfect brotherhood of believers in the Buddha and Dharma.

We speak of Buddhahood, the Dharma and the Brotherhood as though they are three different things, but they are really only one. Buddha is manifested in His Dharma and is realised by the Brotherhood. Therefore, to believe in the Dharma and to cherish the Brotherhood is to have faith in the Buddha, and to have faith in the Buddha means to believe in the Dharma and to cherish the Brotherhood.

Therefore, people are emancipated and enlightened simply by having faith in the Buddha. Buddha is the perfectly Enlightened One and He loves everyone as though each were His only child. So if anyone regards Buddha as his own parent, he identifies himself with Buddha and attains Enlightenment.

Those who thus regard Buddha will be supported by His wisdom and perfumed by His grace.

3.   Nothing in the world brings greater benefit than to believe in Buddha. Just hearing Buddha's name, believing and being pleased even for a moment, is incomparably rewarding.

Therefore, one must please oneself by seeking the teachings of Buddha in spite of the conflagration that fills all the world.

It will be hard to meet a teacher who can explain the Dharma; it will be harder to meet a Buddha; but it will be hardest to believe in His teachings.

But now that you have met the Buddha, who is hard to meet, and have had it explained to you what is hard to hear, you ought to rejoice and believe and have faith in Buddha.

4.   On the long journey of human life, faith is the best of companions; it is the best refreshment on the journey; and it is the greatest possession.

Faith is the hand that receives the Dharma; it is the pure hand that receives all the virtues. Faith is the fire that consumes all the impurities of worldly desires, it removes the burden, and it is the guide that leads one's way.

Faith removes greed, fear and pride; it teaches courtesy and to respect others; it frees one from the bondage of circumstances; it gives one courage to meet hardship; it gives one power to overcome temptations; it enables one to keep one's deeds bright and pure; and it enriches the mind with wisdom.

Faith is the encouragement when one's way is long and wearisome, and it leads to Enlightenment.

Faith makes us feel that we are in the presence of Buddha and it brings us to where Buddha's arm supports us. Faith softens our hard and selfish minds and gives us a friendly spirit and a mind of understanding sympathy.

5. Those who have faith gain the wisdom to recognise the Buddha's teachings in whatever they hear. Those who have faith gain the wisdom to see that everything is but the appearance that arises from the law of causes and conditions, and then faith gives them the grace of patient acceptance and the ability to conform to their conditions peacefully.

Faith gives them the wisdom to recognise the transiency of life and the grace not to be surprised or grieved at whatever comes to them or with the passing of life itself, knowing that, however conditions and appearances may change, the truth of life remains always unchanged.

Faith has three significant aspects: repentance, a rejoicing and sincere respect for the virtues of others, and a grateful acceptance of Buddha's appearance.

People should cultivate these aspects of faith; they should be sensitive to their failings and impurities; they should be ashamed of them and confess them; they should diligently practise the recognition of the good traits and good deeds of others and praise them for their sake; and they should habitually desire to act with Buddha and to live with Buddha.

The mind of faith is the mind of sincerity; it is a deep mind, a mind that is sincerely glad to be led to Buddha's Pure Land by His power.

Therefore, Buddha gives a power to faith that leads people to the Pure Land, a power that purifies them, a power that protects them from self-delusion. Even if they have faith only for a moment, when they hear Buddha's name praised all over the world, they will be led to His Pure Land.

6. Faith is not something that is added to the worldly mind – it is the manifestation of the mind's Buddha nature. One who understands Buddha is a Buddha himself; one who has faith in Buddha is a Buddha himself.

But it is difficult to uncover and recover one's Buddha nature; it is difficult to maintain a pure mind in the constant rise and fall of greed, anger and worldly passion; yet faith enables one to do it.

Within the forest of the poisonous Eranda trees are said to grow, but not the fragrant Chandana (sandalwood). It is a miracle if a Chandana (sandalwood) tree grows in an Eranda forest. Likewise, it is often a miracle that faith in Buddha grows in the heart of the people

Therefore, the faith to believe in Buddha is called a "rootless" faith. That is, it has no root by which it can grow in the human mind, but it has a root to grow in the compassionate mind of Buddha.

7. Thus faith is fruitful and sacred. But faith is hard to awaken in an idle mind. In particular, there are five doubts that lurk in the shadows of the human mind and tend to discourage faith.

First, there is doubt in the Buddha's wisdom; second, there is doubt in the Buddha's teachings; third, there is doubt in the person who explains the Buddha's teachings; fourth, there is doubt as to whether the ways and methods suggested for following the Noble Path are reliable; and fifth, there is a person who, because of his arrogant and impatient mind, may doubt the sincerity of others who understand and follow the Buddha's teachings.

Indeed, there is nothing more dreadful than doubt. Doubt separates people. It is a poison that disintegrates friendships and breaks up pleasant relations. It is a thorn that irritates and hurts; it is a sword that kills.

The beginnings of faith were long ago planted by the compassion of Buddha. When one has faith, one should realise this fact and be very grateful to Buddha for His goodness.

One should never forget that it is not because of one's own compassion that one has awakened faith, but because of the Buddha's compassion which long ago threw its pure light of faith human minds and dispelled the darkness of their ignorance. He who enjoys the present faith has entered into their heritage.

Even living an ordinary life, one can be born in the Pure Land, if he awakens faith through the Buddha's long continued compassion.

It is, indeed, hard to be born in this world. It is hard to hear the Dharma; it is harder to awaken faith; therefore, everyone should try one's best to hear the Buddha's teachings.

IV

Sacred Sayings

1. "He abused me, he laughed at me, he struck me." Thus one thinks and so long as one retains such thoughts one's anger continues.

Anger will never disappear so long as there are thoughts of resentment in the mind. Anger will disappear just as soon as thoughts of resentment are forgotten.

If a roof is improperly made or in disrepair, rain will leak into the house; so greed enters the mind that is improperly trained or out of control.

To be idle is a short road to death and to be diligent is a way of life; foolish people are idle, wise people are diligent.

An arrow-maker tries to make his arrows straight; so a wise man tries to keep his mind straight.

A disturbed mind is forever active, jumping hither and thither, and is hard to control; but a tranquil mind is peaceful; therefore, it is wise to keep the mind under control.

It is a man's own mind, not his enemy or foe, that lures him into evil ways.

The one who protects his mind from greed, anger and foolishness, is the one who enjoys real and lasting peace.

2. To utter pleasant words without practising them is like a fine flower without fragrance.

The fragrance of a flower does not float against the wind; but the honour of a good man goes even against the wind into the world.

A night seems long to a sleepless man and a journey seems long to a weary traveller; so the time of delusion and suffering seems long to a man who does not know the right teaching.

On a trip a man should travel with a companion of equal mind or one who has a better mind; one had better travel alone than to travel with a fool.

An insincere and evil friend is more to be feared than a wild beast; a wild beast may wound your body, but an evil friend will wound your mind.

So long as a man cannot control his own mind, how can he get any satisfaction from thinking such thoughts as, "This is my son" or "This is my treasure"? A foolish man suffers from such thoughts.

To be foolish and to recognise that one is a fool, is better than to be foolish and imagine that one is wise.

A spoon cannot taste the food it carries. Likewise, a foolish man cannot understand the wise man's wisdom even if he associates with a sage.

Fresh milk is often slow to curdle; so sinful actions do not always bring immediate results. Sinful actions are more like coals of fire that are hidden in the ashes and keep on smouldering, finally causing a greater fire.

A man is foolish to desire privileges, promotion, profits, or honour, for such desires can never bring happiness but will bring suffering instead.

A good friend who points out mistakes and imperfections and rebukes evil is to be respected as if he reveals the secret of some hidden treasure.

3. A man who is pleased when he receives good instruction will sleep peacefully, because his mind is thereby cleansed.

A carpenter seeks to make his beam straight; an arrow-maker seeks to make his arrows well-balanced; the digger of an irrigation ditch seeks to make the water run smoothly; so a wise man seeks to control his mind so that it will function smoothly and truly.

A great rock is not disturbed by the wind; the mind of a wise man is not disturbed by either honour or abuse.

To conquer oneself is a greater victory than to conquer thousands in a battle.

To live a single day and hear a good teaching is better than to live a hundred years without knowing such teaching.

Those who respect themselves must be on constant guard lest they yield to evil desires. Once in a lifetime, at least, they should awaken faith, either in their youth, or in middle age, or even in old age.

The world is always burning, with the fires of greed, anger and foolishness; one should flee from such dangers as soon as possible.

The world is like a bubble, it is like the gossamer web of a spider, it is like the defilement in a dirty jar; one should constantly protect the purity of his mind.

4. To avoid any evil, to seek the good, to keep the mind pure: this is the essence of Buddha's teachings.

Endurance is one of the most difficult disciplines, but it is to him who endures that the final victory comes.

One must remove resentment when he is feeling resentful; one must remove sorrow while he is in the midst of sorrow;

one must remove greediness while he is steeped in greed. To live a pure unselfish life, one must count nothing as one's own in the midst of abundance.

To be healthy is a great advantage; to be contented with what one has is better than the possession of great wealth; to be considered reliable is the truest mark of friendliness; to attain Enlightenment is the highest happiness.

When one has the feeling of dislike for evil, when one feels tranquil, when one finds pleasure in listening to good teachings, when one has these feelings and appreciates them, one is free of fear.

Do not become attached to the things you like, do not maintain aversion to the things you dislike. Sorrow, fear and bondage come from one's likes and dislikes.

5. Rust grows from iron and destroys it; so evil grows from the mind of man and destroys him.

A scripture that is not read with sincerity soon becomes covered with dust; a house that is not fixed when it needs repairing becomes filthy; so an idle man soon becomes defiled.

Impure acts defile a person; stinginess defiles an offering; so evil acts defile not only this life but also the following lives.

But the defilement to be most dreaded is the defilement of ignorance. A man cannot hope to purify either his body or mind until ignorance is removed.

It is easy to slip into shamelessness, to be pert and bold like a crow, to hurt others without any feeling of regret for such action.

It is hard, indeed, to feel humble, to know respect and honour, to get rid of all attachments, to keep pure in thought and deed, and to become wise.

It is easy to point out the mistakes of others, while it is hard to admit one's own mistakes. A man broadcasts the sins of others without thinking, but he hides his own sins as a gambler hides his extra dice.

The sky holds no trace of bird or smoke or storm; an evil teachings carries no Enlightenment; nothing in this world is stable; but an Enlightened mind is undisturbed.

6. As a knight guards his castle gate, so one must guard one's mind from dangers outside and dangers inside; one must not neglect it for a moment.

Everyone is the master of himself, he is the oasis he can depend on; therefore, everyone should control himself above all.

The first steps toward spiritual freedom from the worldly bonds and fetters are to control one's mind, to stop idle talk, and to be somewhat pensive.

The sun makes the day bright, the moon makes the night beautiful, discipline adds to the dignity of a warrior; so quiet meditation distinguishes the seeker for Enlightenment.

He who is unable to guard his five senses of eyes, ears, nose, tongue and body, and becomes tempted by his surroundings, is not the one who can train for Enlightenment. He who firmly guards the gateways of his five senses and keeps his mind under control is the one who can successfully train for Enlightenment.

7. He who is influenced by his likes and dislikes cannot rightly understand the significance of circumstances and tends to be overcome by them; he who is free from attachments rightly understands circumstances and to him all things become new and significant.

Happiness follows sorrow, sorrow follows happiness, but when one no longer discriminates between happiness and sorrow, a good deed and a bad deed, one is able to realise freedom.

To worry in anticipation or to cherish regret for the past is like the reeds that are cut and wither away.

The secret of health for both mind and body is not to mourn for the past, not to worry about the future, or not anticipate troubles, but to live wisely and earnestly for the present.

Do not dwell in the past, do not dream of the future, concentrate the mind on the present moment.

It is worthy to perform the present duty well and without failure; do not seek to avoid or postpone it till tomorrow. By acting now, one can live a good day.

Wisdom is the best guide and faith is the best companion. One must try to escape from the darkness of ignorance and suffering, and seek the light of Enlightenment.

If a man's body and mind are under control he should give evidence of it in virtuous deeds. This is a sacred duty. Faith will then be his wealth, sincerity will give his life a sweet savour, and to accumulate virtues will be his sacred task.

In life's journey faith is nourishment, virtuous deeds are a shelter, wisdom is the light by day and right -mindedness is the protection by night. If a man lives a pure life nothing can limit his freedom.

One should forget oneself for the sake of one's family; one should forget one's family for the sake of one's village; one should forget one's village for the sake of the nation; and one should forget everything for the sake of Enlightenment.

Everything is changeable, everything appears and disappears; there is no blissful peace until one passes beyond the agony of life and death.

Part – IV
THE BROTHERHOOD

Part – IV

THE BROTHERHOOD

Chapter One

Duties of the Brotherhood

I

Homeless Brothers

1. A man who wishes to become my disciple must be willing to give up all direct relations with his family, the social life of the world and all dependence upon wealth.

A man who has given up all such relations for the sake of the Dharma and has no abiding place for either his body or mind has become my disciple and is to be called a homeless brother.

Though his feet leave their imprints in my footsteps and his hands carry my garment, if his mind is disturbed by greed, he is far from me. Though he dresses like a monk, if he does not accept the teachings, he does not see me.

But if he has removed all greed and his mind is pure and peaceful, he is very close to me though he be thousands of miles away. If he receives the Dharma, he will see me in it.

2. My disciples, the homeless brothers must observe the four rules and build their lives upon them.

First, they wear old and cast-off garments; second, they get their food through alms-begging; third, their home is where night finds them as under a tree or on a rock; and, fourth, they use only a special medicine made from urine laid down by the Brotherhood.

To carry a bowl in the hand and go from house to house is a beggar's life, but a brother is not compelled to do so by others, he is not forced into it by circumstances or by temptation; he does it of his own free will because he knows that a life of faith will keep him away from the delusions of life, will help him to avoid suffering, and will lead him toward Enlightenment.

The life of a homeless brother is not an easy one; he ought not to undertake it if he cannot keep his mind free from greed and anger or if he cannot control his mind or his five senses.

3. He who believes himself to be a homeless brother and to be able to answer when he is asked about it, must be able to say:

"I am willing to undertake whatever is necessary to be a homeless brother. I will be sincere about it and will try to accomplish the purpose for becoming one. I will be grateful to those who help me by donations and will try to make them happy by my earnestness and good life."

To be a homeless brother he must train himself in many ways: he must be sensitive to shame and dishonour when he fails; he must keep his body, speech and mind pure if his life is to be pure; he must guard the gates of his five senses; he must not lose control of his mind for the sake of some passing pleasure; he must not praise himself or rebuke others; and he must not be idle or given to lengthy sleep.

In the evening he should have a time for quiet sitting and meditation and a short walk before retiring. For peaceful sleep he should rest on the right side with his feet together and his last thought should be of the time when he wishes to rise in the early morning. Early in the morning he should have another time for quiet sitting and meditation and a short walk afterwards.

During the whole day he should always maintain an alert mind, keeping both body and mind under control, resisting all tendency towards greed, anger, foolishness, sleepiness, inattention, regret, suspicion, and all worldly desires.

Thus, with his mind concentrated, he should cultivate excellent wisdom and aim only at perfect Enlightenment.

4. If a homeless brother forgetting himself, lapses into greed, anger, resentment, jealousy, conceit, self-praise, or insincerity, he is like one carrying a keen two-edged sword, covered only by a thin cloth.

He is not a homeless brother simply because he wears a monk's rags and carries a begging bowl; he is not a homeless brother just because he recites scriptures easily; he is only a man of straw and nothing more.

Even if his external appearance is that of a monk, he can not remove his worldly desires. He is not a homeless brother; he is no more than an infant clothed in a monk's robe.

Those who are able to concentrate and control the mind, who contain wisdom, who have removed all worldly desires, and whose only purpose is to attain Enlightenment – only they can be called the true homeless brothers.

A true homeless brother determines to reach his goal of Enlightenment even though he loses his last drop of blood and his bones crumble into powder. Such a man, trying his best, will finally attain the goal and give evidence of it by his ability to do the meritorious deeds of a homeless brother.

5. The mission of a homeless brother is to carry forward the light of the Buddha's teachings. He must preach to everyone; he must wake up sleeping people; he must correct false ideas; he must help people have a right viewpoint; he must go everywhere to spread the teachings even at the risk of his own life.

The mission of a homeless brother is not an easy one, so he who aspires to it should wear Buddha's clothes, sit on Buddha's seat and enter into Buddha's room.

To wear Buddha's clothes means to be humble and to practise endurance; to sit on Buddha's seat means to see matter as non-substantial and to have no attachments; to enter into Buddha's room means to share His all-embracing great compassion and to have sympathy for everyone.

6. Those who wish to teach the Buddha's teachings acceptably must be concerned about four things: first, they must be concerned about their own behaviour; second, they must be concerned about their choice of words when they approach and teach people; third, they must be concerned about their motive for teaching and the end they wish to accomplish; and fourth, they must be concerned about the great compassion.

Firstly, to be a good teacher of the Dharma, then, a homeless brother must first of all have his feet well set on the ground of endurance; he must be modest; he must not be extreme or desire publicity; he must constantly think of the emptiness of things; and he must not become attached to anything. If he is thus concerned he will be capable of right conduct.

Secondly, he must exercise caution in approaching people and situations. He must avoid people who are living evil lives or people of authority; he must avoid opposite sex. Then he must approach people in a friendly way; he must always remember that things rise from a combination of causes and conditions, and, standing at that point, he must not blame or abuse them, or speak of their mistakes, or hold them in light esteem.

Thirdly, he must keep his mind peaceful, considering Buddha as his spiritual father, considering other homeless brothers who are training for Enlightenment as his teachers, and looking upon everyone with great compassion. Then he must teach all equally.

Fourthly, he must let his spirit of compassion display itself, even as Buddha did, to the utmost degree. Especially he should let his spirit of compassion flow out to those who do not know enough to seek Enlightenment. He should wish that they might seek Enlightenment, and then he should follow his wishes with unselfish effort to awaken their interest.

II

Lay Followers

1. It has already been explained that to become a disciple of Buddha one must believe in the three treasures: the Buddha, the Dharma, and the Samgha.

To become a lay follower one must have an unshakeable faith in Buddha, must believe in His teachings, study and put precepts into practice, and must cherish the Brotherhood.

Lay followers should follow the five precepts: not to kill, not to steal, not to commit adultery, not to lie or deceive, and not to use intoxicants.

Lay followers should not only believe in the three treasures and keep the precepts by themselves, but also they should, as far as they are able, help others observe them, especially their relatives and friends, trying to awaken in them an unshakeable faith in the Buddha, the Dharma and the Samgha, so that they, too, may share in Buddha's compassion.

Lay followers should always remember that the reason they believe in the three treasures and keep the precepts is to enable themselves ultimately to attain Enlightenment, and for that reason they should, though living in the world of desires, avoid becoming attached to such desires.

Lay followers should always keep in mind that sooner or later they will be obliged to part with their parents and families and pass away from this life of birth and death; therefore, they should not become attached to things of this life but should set their minds on the world of Enlightenment, wherein nothing passes away.

2. If lay followers want to awaken an earnest and undisturbed faith in the Buddha's teachings, they should realise within their minds a quiet and undisturbed happiness, that will shine out on all their surroundings and will be reflected back to them.

This mind of faith is pure and gentle, always patient and enduring, arguing, never causing suffering to others but always pondering the three treasures: the Buddha, the Dharma and the Samgha. Thus happiness spontaneously rises in their minds, and the light for Enlightenment can be found everywhere.

Since they are resting in the bosom of Buddha by faith, they are kept far from having a selfish mind, from attachment to their possessions, and, therefore, they have no fear in their daily life or dread of being criticized.

They will have no fear about their future death since they believe in the birth in Buddha's Land. Since they have faith in the truth and the holiness of the teachings, they can express their thoughts freely and without fear.

Since their minds are filled with compassion for all people, they will make no distinctions among them but will treat all alike, and since their minds are free from likes and dislikes it will be pure and equitable and happy for them to do any good deed.

Whether they live in adversity or in prosperity, it will make no difference to the increase of their faith. If they cherish humility, if they respect the Buddha's teachings, if they are consistent in speech and action, if they are guided by wisdom, if their mind is as immovable as a mountain, then they will make steady progress on the path to Enlightenment.

And though they are forced to live in a difficult situation and among people of impure minds, if they cherish faith in Buddha they can ever lead them toward better deeds.

3. Therefore, one should first have the wish of hearing the Buddha's teachings.

If anyone should tell him that it would be necessary for him to go through fire to gain Enlightenment, then he should be willing to pass through such a fire.

There is satisfaction in hearing the Buddha's name, that is worth passing through a world filled with fires.

If one wishes to follow the Buddha's teachings one must not be egoistic or self-willed, but should cherish feelings of goodwill toward all alike; one should respect those who are worthy of respect; one should serve those who are worthy of service and treat everyone with uniform kindness.

Thus, lay followers are to train their own minds first and not be disturbed by the actions of others. In this manner, they are to receive the Buddha's teachings and put it into practice, not envying others, not being influenced by others, and not considering other ways.

Those who do not believe in the Buddha's teachings have a narrow vision and, consequently, a disturbed mind. But those who believe in the Buddha's teachings, believe that there is a great wisdom and a great compassion embracing everything and, in that faith, they are undisturbed by trifles.

4. Those who hear and receive the Buddha's teachings know that their lives are transient and that their bodies are merely the aggregation of sufferings and the source of all evils, and so they do not become attached to them.

At the same time, they do not neglect to take good care of their bodies, not because they wish to enjoy the physical pleasures of the body, but because the body is temporarily necessary for the attainment of wisdom and for their mission of explaining the path to others.

If they do not take good care of their bodies they cannot live long. If they do not live long, they cannot practise the teachings personally or transmit it to others.

The disciples of Buddha must wear clothing to protect the body from extremes of heat and cold and to cover its private parts, and should not wear it for decoration.

They must eat food to nourish the body so that they may hear and receive and explain the teachings, but they should not eat for mere enjoyment.

They must live in the house of Enlightenment to be protected from the thieves of worldly passions and from the storms of evil teaching, and they should use the house for its real purpose and not for display or the concealment of selfish practices.

Thus, one should value things and use them solely in their relation to Enlightenment and the teachings. He should not possess them or become attached to them for selfish reasons but only as they serve a useful purpose in carrying the teachings to others.

Therefore, his mind should always dwell on the teachings even when he is living with his family. He should care for them with a wise and sympathetic mind, seeking various means to awaken faith in their minds.

5. Lay members of the Buddha's Samgha should study the following lessons every day: How to serve their parents, how to live with their wives and children, how to control themselves, and how to serve Buddha.

To best serve their parents they must learn to practise kindness toward all animate life. To live happily with their wives and children they must keep away from lust and thoughts of selfish comfort.

While hearing the music of the family life they must not forget the sweeter music of the teachings, and while living in the shelter of the home, they should often seek the safer shelter of Zen practice, where wise men find refuge from all impurity and all disturbance.

When laymen are giving offering they should remove all greed from their hearts; when they are in the midst of crowds, their minds should be in the company of wise men; when they face misfortune, they should keep their minds tranquil and free from hindrances.

When they take refuge in the Buddha, they should seek His wisdom.

When they take refuge in the Dharma, they should seek its truth which is like a great ocean of wisdom.

When they take refuge in the Samgha, they should seek its peaceful fellowship unobstructed by selfish interests.

When they wear clothes, they must not forget to put on also the garment of goodness and humility.

When they want to relieve themselves, they must wish to discharge all greed, anger and foolishness from their minds.

When they are toiling on an uphill road, they should think of it as the road to Enlightenment that will carry them beyond the world of delusion. When they are following an easy road, they should take advantage of its easier conditions to make greater progress toward Buddhahood.

When they see a bridge, they must wish to construct the bridge of the teachings to let the people cross.

When they meet a sorrowful man, they should lament the bitterness of this ever-changing world.

When they see a greedy man, they should have a great longing to keep from the illusions of this life and to attain the true riches of Enlightenment.

When they see savoury food, they must be on guard; when they see distasteful food, they should wish that greed might never return.

During the intense heat of summer, they must wish to be away from the heat of worldly desires and gain the fresh coolness of Enlightenment. During the unbearable cold of winter, they must think of the warmth of Buddha's great compassion.

When they recite the sacred scriptures, they should be determined not to forget them and resolve to put their teaching into practice.

When they think of Buddha, they should cherish a deep wish to have eyes like Buddha.

As they fall asleep at night, they should wish that their body, speech and mind might be purified and refreshed; when they awake in the morning, their first wish should be that during that day their minds might be clear to understand all things.

6. Those who follow the teachings of Buddha, because they understand that everything is characterised by "non-substantiality", do not treat lightly the things that enter into a

man's life, but they receive them for what they are and then try to make them fit tools for Enlightenment.

They must not think that this world is meaningless and filled with confusion, while the world of Enlightenment is full of meaning and peace. Rather, they should taste the way of Enlightenment in all the affairs of this world.

If a man looks upon the world with defiled eyes dimmed by ignorance, he will see it filled with error; but if he looks upon it with clear wisdom, he will see it as the world of Enlightenment, which it is.

The fact is there is only one world, not two worlds, one meaningless and other full of meaning, or one good and the other bad. People only think there are two worlds, due to their discriminating faculty.

If they could rid themselves of these discriminations and keep their minds pure with the light of wisdom, then they would see only one world in which everything is meaningful.

7.   Those who believe in Buddha taste this universal purity of oneness in everything, and in that mind they feel compassion for all and have a humble attitude to serve everyone.

Therefore, they should cleanse their minds of all pride and cherish humility, courtesy and service. Their minds should be like the fruitful earth that nourishes everything without partiality, that serves without complaint, that endures patiently, that is always zealous, that finds, its highest joy in serving all poor people by planting in their minds the seeds of the Buddha's teachings.

Thus, the mind that has compassion for poor people, becomes a mother to all people, honours all people, looks upon all as personal friends, and respects them as parents.

Therefore, though thousands of people may have hard feelings and cherish ill-will toward Buddhist lay followers, they can do no harm, for such harm is like a drop of poison in the waters of a great ocean.

8. A lay follower will enjoy his happiness by habits of recollection, reflection and thanksgiving. He will come to realise that his faith is Buddha's compassion itself and that it has been bestowed upon him by Buddha.

There are no seeds of faith in the mud of worldly passion, but, because of Buddha's compassion, the seeds of faith may be sown there, and they will purify the mind until it has faith to believe in Buddha.

As has been said, the fragrant Chandana (sandalwood) tree cannot grow in a forest of Eranda trees. In like manner, the seeds of faith in Buddha cannot be in the bosom of delusion.

But actually, the flower of joy is blooming there, so we must conclude that while its blossoms are in the bosom of delusion, its roots are elsewhere; namely, its roots are in the bosom of Buddha.

If a lay follower becomes ego-centred, he will become jealous, envious, hateful and harmful, because his mind has become defiled with greed, anger and foolishness. But if he returns to Buddha, he will accomplish even a greater service for Buddha as mentioned above. It is, indeed, beyond any expression.

Chapter Two

Practical Guide to True Way of Living

I

Family Life

1. It is wrong to think that misfortunes come from the east or from the west; they originate within one's own mind. Therefore, it is foolish to guard against misfortunes from the external world and leave the inner mind uncontrolled.

There is a custom that has come down from ancient times that common people still follow. When they get up in the morning, they first wash their face and rinse their mouth, and then they bow in the six directions – to the east, west, south, north, above and below – wishing that no misfortune may come to them from any direction and that they may have a peaceful day.

But it is different in the Buddha's teachings. Buddha teaches that we are to pay respect to the six directions of Truth and then that we are to behave wisely and virtuously and thus prevent all misfortunes.

To guard the gates in these six directions, people are to remove the defilement of the "four deeds", control the "four evil minds", and plug the "six holes" which cause the loss of wealth.

By the "four deeds" it is meant killing, stealing, committing adultery and falsehood.

The "four evil minds" are greed, anger, foolishness and fear.

The "six holes" which cause the loss of wealth are desire for intoxicating drinks and behaving foolishly, staying up late at night and losing the mind in frivolity, indulging in musical and theatre entertainments, gambling, associating with evil companions, and neglecting one's duties.

Now, what are these six directions of Truth? They are east for the way of parents and child, south for the way of teacher and pupil, west for the way of a man and his friend, below for the way of master and servant and above for the way of the disciples of Buddha.

A child should honour his parents and do for them all that he is supposed to do. He should serve them, help them at their labour, cherish the family lineage, protect the family property, and hold memorial services after they have passed away.

The parents should do five things for their children: avoid doing evil, set an example of good deeds, give them an education, arrange for their marriage, and let them inherit the family wealth at a proper time. If the parents and child follow these rules the family will always live in peace.

A pupil should always rise when his teacher enters, wait upon him, follow his instructions well, not neglect an offering for him, and listen respectfully to his teachings.

At the same time, a teacher should act rightly before a pupil and set a good example for him; he should correctly pass on to him the teachings he has learned; he should use good methods and try to prepare the pupil for honours; and he should not forget to protect the pupil from evil in every possible way. If a teacher and his pupil observe these rules, their association will move smoothly.

A husband should treat his wife with respect, courtesy and fidelity. He should leave the housekeeping to her and sometimes provide for her needs, such as accessories. At the same time, a wife should take pains with the housekeeping, manage the servants wisely, maintain her virtue as a good wife. She should not waste her husband's income, and should manage the house properly and faithfully. If these rules are followed, a happy home will be maintained and there will arise no quarrelling.

The rules of friendship mean there should be mutual sympathy between friends, each supplying what the other lacks and trying to benefit the other, always using friendly and sincere words.

One should keep his friend from falling into evil ways, should protect his property and wealth, and should help him in his troubles. If his friend has some misfortune, he should give him a helping hand, even supporting his family, if necessary. In this way, their friendship will be maintained and they will be increasingly happy together.

A master in his dealings with a servant should observe five things: he should assign work that is suitable for the servant's abilities, give him proper compensation, care for him when he is in ill health, share pleasant things with him, and give him the needed rest.

A servant should observe five things: he should get up in the morning before his master and go to bed after him, should always be honest, take pains to do his work well, and try not to bring discredit to his master's name. If these rules are observed, there will be peace and no controversy between the master and the servant.

A disciple of Buddha should see to it that his family observes the teachings of Buddha. They should cherish respect and consideration for their Buddhist teacher, should treat him with courtesy, attend to and observe his instructions, and always have an offering for him.

Then the teacher of Buddha's teachings should rightly understand the teachings, rejecting wrong interpretations, emphasizing the good, and should seek to lead believers along a smooth path. When a family follows this course, keeping the true teaching as its centre, it will thrive happily.

A man who bows in the six directions does not do so in order to escape from external misfortunes. He does it in order to be on his guard to prevent evils from arising within his own mind.

2. A man should recognise among his acquaintances those with whom he should associate and those with whom he should not.

The ones with whom a man should not associate are those who are greedy, clever talkers, flatterers or wasters.

The ones with whom he should associate are those who are helpful, who are willing to share happiness as well as sufferings, who give good advice and who have a sympathetic heart.

A true friend, the one with whom a man may safely associate, will always stick closely to the right way, will worry secretly about his friend's welfare, will console him in misfortune, will offer him a helping hand when he needs it, will keep his secrets, and will always give him good advice.

It is very difficult to find a friend like this, and, therefore, one should try very hard to be a friend like this. As the sun warms the fruitful earth, so a good friend shines in society because of his good deeds.

3. It would be impossible for a son to repay his parents for their gracious kindness, even if he could carry his father on his right shoulder and his mother on his left for one hundred long years.

And even if he could bathe the bodies of his parents in sweet-smelling ointments for a hundred years, serve as an ideal son, gain a throne for them, and give them all the luxuries of the world, still he would not be able to repay them sufficiently for the great indebtedness of gratitude he owes to them.

But if he leads his parents to Buddha and explains the Buddha's teachings to them, and persuades them to give up a wrong course and follow a right one, leading them to give up all greed and enjoy the practice of offering, then he will be more than repaying them.

Buddha's blessing abides in the home where parents are held in respect and esteem.

4. A family is place where minds come in contact with one another. If these minds love one another, the home will be as beautiful as a flower garden. But if these minds get out of harmony with one another, it is like a storm that plays havoc with the garden.

If discord arises within one's family, one should not blame others but should examine one's own mind and follow a right path.

5. Once there was a man of deep faith. His father died when he was young; he lived happily with his mother, and then he took a wife.

At first, they lived happily together and then, because of a small misunderstanding, the wife and her mother-in-law began to dislike each other. This dislike grew until finally the mother left the young couple to live by herself.

After the mother-in-law left, a son was born to the young couple. A rumour reached the mother-in-law that the young wife had said, "My mother-in-law was always annoying me and as long as she lived with us nothing pleasant ever happened; but as soon as she went we had this happy event."

This rumour angered the mother-in-law who exclaimed, "If the husband's mother is chased away from the house and a happy event takes place, then things have come to a pretty pass. Righteousness must have disappeared from the world."

Then the mother shouted, "Now, we must have a funeral of this 'righteousness'." Like a mad woman she went to the cemetery to hold a funeral service.

A god, hearing of this incident, appeared in front of the woman and tried to reason with her, but in vain.

The god then said to her, "If so, I must burn the child and his mother to death. Will that satisfy you?"

Hearing this, the mother-in-law realised her mistake, apologised for her anger, and begged the god to save the lives of the child and his mother. At the same time, the young wife and her husband realised their injustice to the old woman and went to the cemetery to seek her. The god reconciled them and thereafter they lived together as a happy family.

Righteousness is never lost forever unless one casts it away oneself. Righteousness occasionally may seem to disappear but, in fact, it never disappears. When it seems to be disappearing, it is because one is losing the righteousness of one's own mind.

Discordant minds often bring disaster. A trifling misunderstanding may be followed by great misfortune. This is especially to be guarded against in family life.

6. In family life, the question as to how the daily expenses are to be met always requires the utmost care. Every member must work hard like the diligent ants and the busy bees. No one must rely upon the industry of others, or expect their charity.

On the other hand, a man must not consider what he has earned as totally his own. Some of it must be shared with others, some of it must be saved for an emergency, some of it must be set aside for the needs of the community and the nation, and some of it must be devoted to the needs of the religious teachers.

One should always remember that nothing in the world can strictly be called "mine". What comes to a person comes to him because of a combination of causes and conditions; it can be kept by him only temporarily and, therefore, he must not use it selfishly or for unworthy purposes.

7. When Syamavati, the queen-consort of King Udayana, offered Ananda five hundred garments, Ananda received them with great satisfaction.

The king, hearing of it, suspected Ananda of dishonesty, so he went to Ananda and asked what he was going to do with these five hundred garments.

Ananda replied: "Oh, king, many of the brothers are in rags; I am going to distribute the garments among the brothers."

"What will you do with the old garments?"

"We will make bedcovers out of them."

"What will you do with the old bedcovers?"

"We will make pillowcases."

"What will you do with the old pillowcases?"

"We will make floor-covers out of them."

"What will you do with the old floor-covers?"

"We will use them for foot-towels."

"What will you do with the old foot-towels?"

"We will use them for floor-mops."

"What will you do with the old mops?"

"Your Highness, we will tear them into pieces, mix them with mud and use the mud to plaster the house walls."

Every article entrusted to us must be used with good care in some useful way, because it is not "ours" but is only entrusted to us temporarily.

II

The Life of Women

1. There are four types of women. Of the first type there are those who become angry for slight causes, who have changeable minds, who are greedy and jealous of others' happiness, and who have no sympathy for the needs of others.

Of the second type there are those who grow angry over trifling affairs, who are fickle and greedy, but who do not feel envious of others' happiness and who are sympathetic for the needs of others.

Of the third type there are those who are more broadminded and do not become angry very often, who know how to control a greedy mind but are not able to avoid feelings of jealousy, and who are not sympathetic for the needs of others.

Of the fourth type there are those who are broadminded, who can restrain feelings of greed and retain calmness of mind, who do not feel envious of others' happiness, and who are sympathetic for the needs of others.

2. When a young woman marries, she should make the following resolutions: "I must honour and serve the parents of my husband. They have given us all the advantages we have and are our wise protectors, so I must serve them with appreciation and be ready to help them whenever I can.

"I must be respectful to my husband's teacher because he has given my husband a sacred teaching and we could not live as human beings without the guidance of these sacred teachings.

"I must cultivate my mind so that I will be able to understand my husband and be able to help him in his work. I must never be indifferent to his interests, thinking they are only his affairs and not mine.

"I must study the nature, ability and taste of each of the servants of our family and look after them kindly. I will conserve the income of my husband and will not waste it for any selfish purpose."

3. The relation of husband and wife was not designed merely for their convenience. It has a deeper significance than the mere association of two physical bodies in one house. Husband and wife should take advantage of the intimacies of their association to help each other in training their minds in the holy teaching.

And old couple, an "ideal couple" as they were called, once came to Buddha and said, "Lord, we were married after we had been acquainted in childhood and there has never been a cloud in our happiness. Please tell us if we can be remarried in the next life."

The Buddha gave them this wise answer: "If you both have exactly the same faith, if you both received the teachings in exactly the same way, if you perform charity in the same way and if you have the same wisdom, then you will have the same mind in the next birth."

4. Sujata, the young wife of the eldest son of the rich merchant, Anathapindada, was arrogant, did not respect others and did not listen to the instruction of her husband and his parents and, consequently, some discord arose in the family.

One day the Blessed One came to visit Anathapindada and noticed this state of affairs. He called the young wife, Sujata, and spoke to her kindly, saying:

"Sujata, there are seven types of wives. There is a wife who is like a murderer. She has an impure mind, does not honour her husband and, consequently, turns her heart to another man.

"There is a wife who is like a thief. She never understands her husband's labour but thinks only of her desire for luxury. She wastes her husband's income to satisfy her own appetite and, by so doing, steals from him.

"There is a wife who is like a master. She rails at her husband, neglects the housekeeping and always scolds him with rough words.

"There is a wife who is like a mother. She cares for her husband as though he were a child, protects him as a mother and takes good care of his income.

"There is a wife who is like a sister. She is faithful to her husband and serves him like a sister with modesty and reserve.

"There is a wife who is like a friend. She tries to please her husband as if he were a friend who had just returned from a long absence. She is modest, behaves correctly and treats him with great respect.

"Lastly, there is a wife who is like a maidservant. She serves her husband well and with fidelity. She respects him, obeys his commands, has no wishes of her own, no ill-feeling, no resentment, and always tries to make him happy."

The Blessed One asked, "Sujata, which type of wife are you like, or would you wish to be like?"

Hearing these words of the Blessed One, she was ashamed of her past conduct and replied that she would wish to be like the one in the last example, the maidservant. She changed her behaviour and became her husband's helper, and together they sought Enlightenment.

5. Amrapali was a wealthy and famous courtesan of Vaisali and kept many young and beautiful prostitutes with her. She called upon the Blessed One and asked Him to give her some good teaching.

The Blessed One said, "Amrapali, the mind of a woman is easily disturbed and misled. She yields to her desires and surrenders to jealousy more easily than a man.

"Therefore, it is more difficult for a woman to follow the Noble Path. This is especially true for a young and beautiful woman. You must step forth toward the Noble Path by overcoming lust and temptation.

"Amrapali, you must remember that youth and beauty do not last but are followed by sickness, old age and suffering. Desires for wealth and love are women's besetting temptations, but, Amrapali, they are not the eternal treasures. Enlightenment is the only treasure that maintains its value. Strength is followed by illness; youth must yield to old age; life gives way to death. One may have to go away from a loved one to live with a hated one; one may not obtain what one wishes for very long. This is the law of life.

"The only thing that protects and brings one to lasting peace is Enlightenment. Amrapali, you should seek Enlightenment at once."

She listened to Him, became his disciple and, as an offering, donated to the Brotherhood her beautiful garden park.

6. There are no distinctions of sex on the path to Enlightenment. If a woman makes up her mind to seek Enlightenment, she becomes a heroine of the True Path.

Mallika, the daughter of King Prasenajit and the queen of King Ayodhya, was such a heroine. She had great faith in the teachings of the Blessed One and made in His presence the ten following vows:

"My Lord, until I gain Enlightenment I will not violate the sacred precepts; I will not be arrogant before people who are older than myself; I will not become angry with anyone.

"I will not be jealous of others or envy their possessions; I will not be selfish either in mind or property; I will try to make poor people happy with the things I receive and will not hoard them for myself.

"I will receive all people courteously, give them what they need, and speak kindly to them; consider their circumstances and not my convenience; and try to benefit them without partiality.

"If I see others in solitude, in prison, suffering from disease or other troubles, I will try to relieve them and make them happy, by explaining the reasons and laws to them.

"If I see others catching living animals and being cruel to them or violating any such precept, I will punish them if they are to be punished, or teach them if they are to be taught, and then I will try to undo what they have done and correct their mistakes, to the best of my ability.

"I will not forget to hear the right teaching, for I know that when one neglects the right teaching one quickly falls away from the truth that abides everywhere, and will fail to reach the shore of Enlightenment."

Then she made the following three wishes to save poor people: "First, I will try to make everyone peaceful. This wish, I believe, in whatever life I may hereafter receive, will be the root of goodness that will grow into the wisdom of good teaching.

"Second, after I have received the wisdom of good teaching, I will untiringly teach all people.

"Third, I will protect the true teaching, even at the sacrifice of my own body, life or property."

The true significance of family life is the opportunity it gives for mutual encouragement and aid on the path to Enlightenment. Even an ordinary woman, if she has the same mind to seek Enlightenment, and makes the same vows and wishes, may become as great a disciple of Buddha as Mallika was.

III

In Service

1. There are seven teachings which lead a country to prosperity: First, people should assemble often to discuss political affairs, and to provide for national defence.

Second, the people of all social classes should meet together in unity to discuss their national affairs.

Third, people should respect old customs and not change them unreasonably, and they should also observe the rules of ceremony and maintain justice.

Fourth, they should recognise the differences of sex and seniority, and maintain the purity of families and communities.

Fifth, they should be filial to their parents and faithful to their teachers and elders.

Sixth, they should honour the ancestors' shrines and keep up the annual rites.

Seventh, they should esteem public morality, honour virtuous conduct, listen to honourable teachers and make offerings to them.

If a country follows these teachings well, it will surely prosper and will be held in respect by all other countries.

2. Once there was a king who was notably successful in ruling his kingdom. Because of his wisdom he was called king Great-Light. He explained the principles of his administration as follows:

The best way for a ruler to reign over his country is first of all to rule himself. A ruler should come before his people with a heart of compassion, and should teach and lead them to remove all impurities from their minds. The happiness that comes from good teachings far exceeds any enjoyment that the material things of the world can offer. Therefore, he could give his people good teaching and keep their minds and bodies tranquil.

When poor people come to him he should open his storehouse and let them take what they want, and then he will take advantage of the opportunity to teach them the wisdom of ridding themselves of all greed and evil.

Each man has a different view of things according to the state of his mind. Some people see the city where they live as fine and beautiful, others see it as dirty and dilapidated. It all depends on the state of their minds.

Those who hold good teachings in respect, can see in common trees and stones all the beautiful lights and colours of lapis lazuli, while greedy people, who do not know enough to control their own minds, are blind even to the splendours of a golden palace.

Everything in the nation's daily life is like that. The mind is the source of everything, and, therefore, the ruler should first seek to have his people train their minds.

3. The first principle in wise' administration is like the principle of king Great-Light: to lead the people to train their minds.

To train the mind means to seek Enlightenment, and, therefore, the wise ruler must give his first attention to the Buddha's teachings.

If a ruler has faith in Buddha, is devoted to His teachings, appreciates and pays tribute to virtuous and compassionate people there will be no favouritism toward either friends or enemies and his country will always remain prosperous.

If a country is prosperous, it is not necessary for it to attack any other country and it does not need any weapons of attack.

When people are happy and satisfied, class differences disappear, good deeds are promoted, virtues are increased, and people come to respect one another. Then everyone becomes prosperous; the weather and temperature become normal; the sun and the moon and stars shine naturally; rains and winds come timely; and all natural calamities disappear.

4. The duty of a ruler is to protect his people. He is the parent of his people and he protects them by his laws. He must raise his people like parents raise their children, giving a dry cloth to replace a wet one without waiting for the child to cry. In like manner, the ruler must remove suffering and bestow happiness without waiting for people to complain. Indeed, his ruling is not perfect until his people abide in peace. They are his country's treasure.

Therefore, a wise ruler is always thinking of his people and does not forget them even for a moment. He thinks of their hardships and plans for their prosperity. To rule wisely he must be advised about everything – about water, about drought, about storm and about rain; he must know about crops, the chances for a good harvest, people's comforts and their sorrows. To be in a position to rightly award, punish or praise, he must be thoroughly informed as to the guilt of bad men and the merits of good men.

A wise ruler gives to his people when they are in need, and collects from them when they are prosperous. He should exercise his correct judgment when collecting taxes and make the levy as light as possible, thus keeping his people consonant.

A wise ruler will protect his people by his power and dignity. One who thus rules one's people is worthy to be called a king.

5. The king of Truth is the king of kings. His ancestry is of the purest and the highest. He not only rules the four quarters of the world, but he is also Lord of Wisdom and Protector of all Virtuous Teachings.

Wherever he goes, fighting ceases and ill-will vanishes. He rules with equity by the power of Truth, and by vanquishing all evil he brings peace to all people.

The king of Truth never slays or steals or commits adultery. He never cheats or abuses or lies or talks idly. His mind is free from all greed, anger and foolishness. He removes these ten evils and in their place establishes the ten virtues.

Because his rule is based upon Truth he is invincible. Wherever Truth appears violence ceases and ill-will vanishes. There is no dissension among his people, and, therefore, they dwell in quietness and safety; his mere presence brings peacefulness and happiness among them. That is why he is called the king of Truth.

Since the king of Truth is the king of kings, all other rulers praise his excellent name and rule their own kingdoms after his example.

Thus the king of Truth is the sovereign over all kings, and under his righteous way they bring safety to their people and fulfil their duties with Dharma.

6. A wise ruler will temper his verdicts with compassion. He will try to consider each case with clear wisdom and then make his verdict in accord with the five principles.

The five principles are:

First, he must examine the truthfulness of the facts presented.

Second, he must ascertain that they fall within his jurisdiction. If he renders a judgment with full authority, it is effective, but if he does so without authority, it only causes complications; he should await the correct conditions.

Third, he must judge justly; that is, he must enter into the mind of the defendant. If he finds that the deed was done without criminal intent, he should discharge the man.

Fourth, he should pronounce his verdict with kindness but not harshness; that is, he should apply a proper punishment but should not go beyond that. A good ruler will instruct a criminal with kindness and give him time to reflect upon his mistakes.

Fifth, he should judge with sympathy but not in anger; that is, he should condemn the crime but not the criminal. He should let his judgment rest upon a foundation of sympathy, and he should use the occasion to try and make the criminal realise his mistakes.

7. If an important minister of state neglects his duties, works for his own profit or accepts bribes, it will cause a rapid decay of public morals. People will cheat one another, a strong man will attack a weaker one, a noble will mistreat a commoner or a wealthy man will take advantage of the poor, and there will be no justice for anyone; mischief will abound and troubles will multiply.

Under such circumstances, faithful ministers will retire from public service, wise men will keep silent from fear of complications, and only flatterers will hold government positions, and they will use their political power to enrich themselves with no thought for the sufferings of the people.

Under such conditions the power of the government becomes ineffective and its righteous policies fall into ruins.

Such unjust officials are the thieves of people's happiness, yet are worse than thieves because they defraud both ruler and people and are the cause of the nation's troubles. The king should root out such ministers and punish them.

But even in a country which is ruled by a good king and by just laws, there is another form of disloyalty. There are sons who give themselves up to the love of their wives and children and forget the grace of their parents who nursed and cared for them during many a year. They neglect their parents, rob them of their possessions and neglect their teaching. Such sons are to be counted among the most wicked of men.

And why? It is because they are unfilial to their parents whose long love has been very great, a love that could not be repaid even if the sons honoured and treated them kindly throughout their lives. Those who are disloyal to their ruler and unfilial to their parents should be punished as the worst of criminals.

And also, in a country which is ruled by a good king and by just laws, there is still another form of disloyalty. There are people who are entirely forgetting the three treasures, the Buddha, the Dharma and the Samgha. Such people destroy their country's sanctuaries, burn the sacred scriptures, make the teachers of righteousness serve them, and thus violate the sacred teachings of Buddha. They are also among the worst of criminals.

And why? It is because they destroy the spiritual faith of their nation, which is its foundation and the source of its virtues. Such people, by burning the faith of others, are digging their own graves.

All other sins may be regarded as light in comparison with these disloyalties. Such disloyal criminals should be punished most severely.

8. There may be a conspiracy against a good king who is ruling his country according to the right teachings, or perhaps foreign enemies may raid the country. In such a case the king should make three decisions.

He should decide:

"First, these conspirators or foreign enemies are threatening the good order and welfare of our country; I must protect the people and country even with armed force.

"Second, I will try to find some way of defeating them without resorting to the use of arms.

"Third, I will try to capture them alive, without killing them if possible, and disarm them."

By adopting these three decisions the king will proceed most wisely, after setting necessary posts and giving instructions.

By proceeding in this way, the country and its soldiers will be encouraged by the king's wisdom and dignity and will respect both his firmness and grace. When it is necessary to call upon the soldiers, they will fully understand the reason for war and its nature. Then they will go to the field of battle with courage and loyalty, respecting the king's wise and gracious sovereignty. Such a war will not only bring victory but also add virtue to the country.

Chapter Three

Building a Buddha Land

I

The Harmony of Brotherhood

1. Let us imagine a desert country lying in absolute darkness with many living things swarming blindly about in it.

Naturally they will be frightened and as they run about without recognising one another during the night, there will be frequent squirming and loneliness. This is indeed a pitiful sight.

Then let us imagine that suddenly a superior man with a torch appears and everything around becomes bright and clear.

The living beings in the dark solitude suddenly find a great relief as they look about to recognise one another and happily share their companionship.

By "a desert country" is meant a world of human life when it lies in the darkness of ignorance. Those who have no light of wisdom in their minds wander about in loneliness and fear. They were born alone and die alone; they do not know how to associate with their fellow-men in peaceful harmony, and they are naturally despondent and fearful.

By "a superior man with torch" is meant Buddha assuming a human form, and by His wisdom and compassion He illumines the world.

In this light people find themselves as well as others and are glad to establish human fellowship and harmonious relations.

Thousands of people may live in a community but it is not one of real fellowship until they know each other and have sympathy for one another.

A true community has faith and wisdom that illuminate it. It is a place where the people know and trust one another and where there is social harmony.

In fact, harmony is the life and real meaning of a true community or an organisation.

2. Of organisations, there are three kinds. First, there are those that are organised on the basis of the power, wealth or authority of great leaders.

Second, there are those that are organised because of its convenience to the members, which will continue to exist as long as the members satisfy their conveniences and do not quarrel.

Third, there are those that are organised with some good teaching as its centre and harmony as its very life.

Of course, the third or last of these is the only true organisation, for in it the members live in one spirit, from which the unity of spirit and various kinds of virtue will arise. In such an organisation there will prevail harmony, satisfaction and happiness.

Enlightenment is like rain that falls on a mountain and gathers into rivulets that run into brooks, and then into rivers which finally flow in the ocean.

The rain of the sacred teachings falls on all people alike without regard to their conditions or circumstances. Those who accept it gather into small groups, then into organisations, then into communities and, finally, find themselves in the great Ocean of Enlightenment.

The minds of these people mix like milk and water and finally organise into a harmonious Brotherhood.

Thus, the true teaching is the fundamental requirement of a perfect organisation and, as mentioned above, it is the light which enables people to recognise one another, to become adjusted to one another and to smooth out the rough places in their thinking.

Thus, the organisation that is formed on the perfect teachings of Buddha can be called a Brotherhood.

They should observe these teachings and train their minds accordingly. Thus, the Buddha's Brotherhood will theoretically include everyone, but, in fact, only those who have the same religious faith are members.

3. The Buddha's Brotherhood will have two types of members: there will be those who are teaching the lay members, and those who are supporting the teachers by offering the needed food and clothing. They together will disseminate and perpetuate the teachings.

Then, to make the Brotherhood complete, there must be perfect harmony among the members. The teachers teach the members and the members honour the teachers so that there can be harmony between them.

Members of the Buddha's Brotherhood should associate together with affectionate sympathy, being happy to live together with fellow-followers, and seeking to become one in spirit.

4. There are six things that will help to lead a Brotherhood to harmony. They are: first, sincerity of speech; second, sincerity and kindness of action; third, sincerity and sympathy of spirit; fourth, equal sharing of common property; fifth, following the same pure precepts; and sixth, all having right views.

Among these things, the sixth or "all having right views" forms the nucleus, with the other five serving as wrapping for it.

There are two sets of seven rules to be followed if the Brotherhood is to be a success. The first is, as a group:

(1) they should gather together frequently to listen to the teachings and to discuss them;

(2) they should mingle freely and respect one another;

(3) they should revere the teachings and respect the rules and not change them;

(4) elder and younger members are to treat each other with courtesy;

(5) they should let sincerity and reverence mark their bearing;

(6) they should purify their minds in a quiet place which they should, nevertheless, offer to others before taking it for themselves;

(7) they should love all people, treat visitors cordially, and console the sick with kindness;

A Brotherhood that follows these rules will never decline.

The second is, individually each should: (1) maintain a pure spirit and not ask for too many things; (2) maintain integrity and remove all greed; (3) be patient and not argue; (4) keep silent and not talk idly; (5) submit to the regulations and not be overbearing; (6) maintain an even mind and not follow different teachings; and (7) be thrifty and frugal in daily living.

If its members follow these rules, the Brotherhood will endure and never decline.

5. As mentioned above, a Brotherhood should maintain harmony in its very essence; therefore, one without harmony cannot be called a brotherhood. Each member should be on guard not to be the cause of discord. If discord appears it should be removed as early as possible, for discord will soon ruin any organisation.

Blood stains cannot be removed by more blood; resentment cannot be removed by more resentment; resentment can be removed only by forgetting it.

6. Once there was a king named Calamity, whose country was conquered by a neighbouring warlike king named Brahmadatta. King Calamity, after hiding with his wife and son for a time, was captured but fortunately his son, the prince, could escape.

The prince tried to find some way of saving his father but in vain. On the day of his father's execution, the prince in disguise made his way into the execution ground where he could do nothing but watch in mortification the death of his ill-fated father.

The father noticed his son in the crowd and muttered as if talking to himself, "Do not search for a long time; do not act hastily; resentment can be calmed only by forgetting it."

Afterward, the prince sought after some way of revenge for a long time. At last he was employed as an attendant in Brahmadatta's palace and came to win the king's favours.

On a day when the king went hunting, the prince sought some opportunity for revenge. The prince was able to lead his master into a lonely place, and the king, being very weary, fell asleep with his head on the lap of the prince, so fully had he come to trust the prince.

The prince drew his dagger and placed it at the king's throat but then hesitated. The words his father had expressed at the moment of his execution flashed into his mind and although he tried again he could not kill the king. Suddenly the king awoke and told the prince that he had had a bad dream in which the son of King Calamity was trying to kill him.

The prince, flourishing the dagger in his hand, hastily grasped the king and, identifying himself as the son of King Calamity, declared that the time had finally come for him to avenge his father. Yet he could not do so, and suddenly he cast his dagger down and fell on his knees in front of the king.

When the king heard the prince's story and the final words of his father, he was very impressed and apologised to the prince. Later, he restored the former kingdom to the prince and their two countries came to live in friendship for a long time.

The dying words of King Calamity, "Do not search for a long time," meant that resentment should not be cherished for long, and "Do not act hastily" meant that friendship should not be broken hastily.

Resentment cannot be satisfied by resentment; it can only be removed by forgetting it.

In the fellowship of a Brotherhood that is based on the Harmony of right teaching, every member should always appreciate the spirit of this story.

Not only the members of the Brotherhood but also people in general should appreciate and practise this spirit in their daily lives.

II

The Buddha's Land

1. As has been explained, if a Brotherhood does not forget its duty of spreading Buddha's teachings and of living in harmony, it will steadily grow larger and its teachings will spread more widely.

This means that more and more people will be seeking Enlightenment, and it also means that the evil armies of greed, anger, and foolishness, which are led by the devil of ignorance and lust, will begin to retreat, and that wisdom, light, faith and joy will dominate.

The devil's dominion is full of greed, darkness, struggle, fight, swords and bloodshed, and is replete with jealousy, prejudice, hatred, cheating, flattery, fawning, secrecy and abuse.

Now suppose that the light of wisdom shines upon the dominion, and the rain of compassion falls upon it, and faith begins to take root, and the blossoms of joy begins to spread their fragrance. Then that devil's domain will turn into Buddha's Pure Land.

And just like a soft breeze and a few blossoms on a branch that tell the coming of spring, so when a man attains Enlightenment, grass, trees, mountains, rivers and all other things begin to throb with new life.

If a man's mind becomes pure, his surroundings will also become pure.

2. In a land where the true teachings prevails, every dweller has a pure and tranquil mind. Indeed, Buddha's compassion untiringly benefits all people, and His shining spirit exorcises all impurities from their minds.

A pure mind soon becomes a deep mind, a mind that is commensurate with the Noble Path, a mind that loves to give, a mind that loves to keep the precepts, an enduring mind, a zealous mind, a calm mind, a wise mind, a compassionate mind, that leads people to Enlightenment by many and skilful means. Thus shall the Buddha's Land be built.

A home with one's wife and children is transformed into a home where Buddha is present; a country that suffers because of social distinctions is likewise transformed into a fellowship of kindred spirits.

A golden place that is bloodstained cannot be the abiding place for Buddha. A small hut where the moonlight leaks in through chinks in the roof can be transformed into a place where Buddha will abide, if the mind of its master is pure.

When a Buddha Land is founded upon the pure mind of a single man, that single pure mind draws other kindred minds to itself in the fellowship of a brotherhood. Faith in Buddha spreads from individual to family, from family to village, from village to towns, to cities, to countries, and finally to the whole worlds.

Indeed, earnestness and faithfulness in spreading the teaching of the Dharma are what build the Buddha Land.

3. To be sure, when viewed from one angle, the world with all its greed and injustice and bloodshed appears as a devil's world; but, as people come to believe in Buddha's Enlightenment, blood will be turned into milk and greed into compassion, and then the devil's land becomes a Buddha Land of Purity.

It seems an impossible task to empty an ocean with a small ladle, but the determination to do it, even if it takes many, many lives, is the mind with which one should receive Buddha's Enlightenment.

Buddha is waiting on the other shore; that is, His world of Enlightenment, wherein there is no greed, no anger, no ignorance, no suffering, no agony, but where there are only the light of wisdom and the rain of compassion.

It is a land of peace, a refuge for those who suffer and who are in sorrow and agony; a place of rest for those who take a break in their spreading of the teachings of the Dharma.

In this Pure Land there are boundless Light and everlasting life. Those who reach this haven will never return to the world of delusion.

Indeed, this Pure Land, where the flowers perfume the air with wisdom and the birds sing the holy Dharma, is the final destination for all mankind.

4.   Though this Pure Land is the place for taking rest, it is not the place for idleness. Its beds of fragrant flowers are not for slothful indolence, but are the places for refreshment and rest, where one regains energy and zeal to continue the Buddha's mission of Enlightenment.

Buddha's mission is everlasting. As long as men live and creatures exist, and as long as selfish and defiled minds create their own worlds and circumstances, there will be no end to His mission.

The children of Buddha, who have crossed to the Pure Land by means of the great power of Amida, may be zealous to return to the land whence they came and where they still have ties. There they will take their part in the Buddha's mission.

As the light of a small candle will spread from one to another in succession, so the light of Buddha's compassion will pass on from one mind to another endlessly.

The children of Buddha, realising His spirit of compassion, adopt His task of Enlightenment and Purification, and pass it on from one generation to another in order to make the Buddha's Land glorified eternally and forever.

III

Those Who Have Received Glory in Buddha's Land

1. Syamavati, the consort of King Udayana, was deeply devoted to Buddha.

She lived in the innermost courts of the palace and did not go out, but her maid, Uttara, who had an excellent memory, used to go out and attend the Buddha's preaching.

On her return, the maid would repeat to the queen the teachings of the Blessed One, and thus the queen deepened her wisdom and faith.

The second wife of the king was jealous of the first wife and sought to kill her. She slandered her to the king until finally he believed her and sought to kill his first wife, Syamavati.

Queen Syamavati stood in front of the king so calmly that he had no heart to kill her. Regaining control of himself he apologised to her for his distrust.

The jealousy of the second wife increased and she sent wicked men to set fire to the innermost courts of the palace during the king's absence from home. Syamavati remained calm, quiet and encouraged the bewildered maids, and then, without fear, died peacefully in the spirit she had learned from the Blessed One. Uttara died with her in the fire.

Among the many women disciples of Buddha, these two were most highly honoured: Queen Syamavati as a compassionate spirit and her maid, Uttara, as a good listener.

2. Prince Mahanama, of the Shakya clan and a cousin of Buddha, had great faith in the teachings of Buddha and was one of his most faithful followers.

At that time a violent king named Virudaka of Kosala conquered the Shakya clan. Prince Mahanama went to the king and sought the lives of his people, but the king would not listen to him. He then proposed that the king would let as many prisoners escape as could run away while he himself remained underwater in a nearby pond.

To this the king assented, thinking that the time would be very short for him to be able to stay underwater.

The gate of the castle was opened as Mahanama dived into the water and the people rushed for safety. But Mahanama did not come up, sacrificing his life for the lives of his people by tying his hair to the underwater root of a willow tree.

3. Utpalavarna was a famous nun whose wisdom was compared with that of Maudgalyayana, a great disciple of Buddha. She was, indeed, the nun of all nuns and was always their leader, never tiring of teaching them.

Devadatta was a very wicked and cruel man who poisoned the mind of King Ajatasatru and persuaded him to turn against the teachings of Buddha. But later, King Ajatasatru repented, broke off his friendship with Devadatta, and became a humble disciple of Buddha.

At one time when Devadatta was repulsed from the castle gate in an attempt to see the king, he met Utpalavarna coming out. It made him very angry, so he struck and seriously wounded her.

She returned to her convent in great pain and when the other nuns tried to console her she said to them: "Sisters, human life is the unforeseen, everything is transient and egoless. Only the world of Enlightenment is tranquil and peaceful. You must keep on with your training." Then she passed away quietly.

4. Angulimalya, once a terrible bandit who had killed many people, was saved by the Blessed One, and he became one of His disciples.

One day he went begging in a town and endured much hardship and suffering for his past evil deeds.

The villagers fell upon him and beat him severely, but he went back to the Blessed One with his body still bleeding, falling at His feet and thanking Him for the opportunity that had come to him to suffer for his former cruel deeds.

He said, "Blessed One, my name originally was 'No Harming,' but because of my ignorance, I took many precious lives, and from each I took a finger; because of that, I came to be called Angulimalya, the collector of fingers!

"Then, through your compassion, I learned wisdom and became devoted to the three treasures of the Buddha, the Dharma and the Samgha. When a man drives a horse or a cow he has to use a whip or a rope, but you, the Blessed One, purified my mind without the use of whip or rope or hook.

"Today, Blessed One, I have suffered only what was my due. I do not wish to live, I do not wish to die. I only wait for my time to come."

5. Maudgalyayana, together with the venerable Sariputra, was one of the Buddha's two greatest disciples. When the teachers of other religions saw that the pure water of the Buddha's teachings was spreading among the people and found the people eagerly drinking it, they became jealous and applied various hindrances to his preaching.

But none of the hindrances could stop or prevent his teachings from spreading widely. The followers of the other religions attempted to kill Maudgalyayana.

Twice he escaped but the third time he was surrounded by many heathens and fell under their blows.

Sustained by Enlightenment, he calmly received their blows, and though his flesh was torn and his bones crushed, he died peacefully.